IF HE LOVES ME ...

Six months ago, ANNIE, 20, ended a two-year relationship with the man to whom she'd lost her virginity. It seemed he always knew exactly where to touch her, and Annie had an orgasm almost every time they had sex. For the last month, she's been dating Mark and has fallen deeply in love with him. But their lovemaking is a disaster. Afraid of wounding his ego, Annie hasn't told Mark what she would enjoy—and so she continues to suffer in silence.

MANDY, 28, has been happily married—and faking orgasm—for six years. She thought she was happy until one of her girl-friends began talking about a new lover and the marvelous climaxes they had reached together. When she heard her friend brag about the fun she was having in bed, she felt left out—and confused. Still, what could she possibly do to change a sexual pattern that had been in place for years?

Now
EVERY WOMAN CAN!

THE NICE GIRL'S GUIDE TO SENSATIONAL SEX

Other **Cosmopolitan Books**

THE 1995 BEDSIDE ASTROLOGER

Look for These
Cosmopolitan Books
Coming Soon

WHAT MEN WANT FROM THE WOMEN THEY LOVE
ALL THE GOOD ONES ARE *NOT* TAKEN

Cosmopolitan Books are available at special quantity discounts for bulk purchases for sales promotions, premiums, fund raising or educational use. Special books, or book excerpts, can also be created to fit specific needs.

For details write or telephone the office of the Director of Special Markets, Avon Books, Dept. FP, 1350 Avenue of the Americas, New York, New York 10019, 1-800-238-0658.

THE NICE GIRL'S GUIDE TO SENSATIONAL SEX

NANCY KALISH

COSMOPOLITAN™

If you purchased this book without a cover, you should be aware that this book is stolen property. It was reported as "unsold and destroyed" to the publisher, and neither the author nor the publisher has received any payment for this "stripped book."

THE NICE GIRL'S GUIDE TO SENSATIONAL SEX is an original publication of Avon Books. This work has never before appeared in book form.

The purpose of this book is to educate and entertain. It is sold with the understanding that the publisher and author are not rendering medical, psychological, or other professional services. The publisher and author shall not be liable or responsible to any person or entity with respect to any loss or damage caused or alleged to be caused directly or indirectly by the information that appears in this book. The names and details of the people whose stories appear in this book have been changed to conceal their identities.

COSMOPOLITAN BOOKS
AVON BOOKS
A division of
The Hearst Corporation
1350 Avenue of the Americas
New York, New York 10019

Copyright © 1994 by Nancy Kalish
Published by arrangement with the author
Library of Congress Catalog Card Number: 94-94077
ISBN: 0-380-77229-9

All rights reserved, which includes the right to reproduce this book or portions thereof in any form whatsoever except as provided by the U.S. Copyright Law. For information address Nine Muses & Apollo Agency, 2 Charlton Street, New York, New York 10014.

First Cosmopolitan Books Printing: September 1994

AVON TRADEMARK REG. U.S. PAT. OFF. AND IN OTHER COUNTRIES, MARCA REGISTRADA, HECHO EN U.S.A.

Printed in the U.S.A.

RA 10 9 8 7 6 5 4 3 2 1

Acknowledgements

I would never have been able to finish (or even start) this book without the generous help of the following people. I want to thank the dozens of women and men who talked so openly with me about the most private part of their lives; Bob Mecoy and Marjorie Braman for believing in me and my project from the beginning; Muriel Kalish, Lionel Kalish, and Elizabeth Nix, for their constant encouragement and astute criticisms; Judith Newman, an extraordinary wordsmith and best friend rolled into one, who kept up my spirits *and* my writing throughout (and saved me from myself more than once); and my husband, Steve, who has made this book—and my life—so much better than it would otherwise have been.

TABLE OF CONTENTS

	Introduction	xi
One:	Ready, Set, Sex! It's Time to Wake Up Your Libido!	1
Two:	In Search of the Big "O"	21
Three:	Six Easy Steps to Sexual Confidence	59
Four:	Fantasy Fun: Naughty *and* Normal	101
Five:	What Men *Really* Want	130
Six:	Love Him, Love His Penis	155
Seven:	Beyond the Basics	175

THE NICE GIRL'S GUIDE TO SENSATIONAL SEX

INTRODUCTION

Variety is the spice of great sex, but many women consider themselves too proper to try anything but the standard positions, too polite to ask for what they truly desire in bed, too timid to explore their fantasies (let alone those of their man)—in other words, too much of a "nice girl" to have anything but a safe, yet *boring* sex life.

How do I know? Because *I'm* a nice girl (and most of my girlfriends are too). And it was only after editing many articles on sex as a senior editor at *Cosmopolitan* that I began to believe I could enjoy myself in bed and still be "nice" out of it, that I opened my mind to the possibility that there might be something wonderful beyond the most basic (and proper) ways to make love—and that those wonderful somethings might actually be wonderful for *me*.

That doesn't mean I became a dominatrix or started swapping spouses with the next-door neighbors. Instead, I set out to discover what my friends and I had been missing by researching and writing this book. I began by consulting sex experts, as well as interviewing dozens of ordinary women and men, to ask them the sorts of questions nice girls have always been afraid to ask, but desperately need to know the answers to. The sorts of questions that can forever change a woman's sex life—and make it the amazing and fulfilling experience that it can be. And I got some great answers.

I found out how to wake up a sleepy libido, several foolproof ways to achieve delicious, almost addictive orgasms (even if you've never had one before), what your sexual fantasies really mean and whether or not you should try to make them a reality, plus what men *really* want in bed—and how to give it to them while maximizing your *own* pleasure.

I even gathered my courage (and my dark glasses) to tour several sex shops, sample their wares, and ask the owners exactly what all those strange-looking gadgets are for, as well as how to buy the best vibrator (the answers appear in Chapter Seven).

While writing this book, I discovered many erotic delights I never would have known about, and I have remained a nice girl, albeit one who's much happier in bed. It *can* be done—and, whether you need to learn how to overcome your inhibitions or perfect your oral sex technique, this book will tell you how to do it. For, as Mae West once wisely said, "Too much of a good thing can be wonderful."

THE NICE GIRL'S GUIDE TO SENSATIONAL SEX

READY, SET, SEX!
It's Time To Wake Up Your Libido!

It's a weekday night around 11 p.m. and Terri has just fallen into bed next to her husband Rich after a harried day at work. She's looking forward to watching the late news, when suddenly Rich's hand reaches out from the other side of the bed and begins caressing her shoulders. As he moves down to her breast, she sighs inwardly. Her limbs feel leaden with exhaustion and even though part of her begins responding to his tender touch and kisses, a bigger part just wants to be left alone.

As his embrace becomes more ardent, Terri does some quick calculations, only to realize that she's turned Rich away for several nights now. In fact, it's been more than a week, maybe two, since they last made love. So Terri gives in, not out of lust, but the fear that her husband will make a fuss—or worse, find *another* woman to satisfy his needs. And, as she reluctantly turns towards him and answers his kisses with her own, her annoyance effectively extinguishes any real erotic response she might have had.

When their bodies finally separate and he falls asleep, the main emotion Terri feels is relief. She didn't have an orgasm, but at least it was over quickly and she can still catch the end of the news.

It may seem like Terri has a serious sexual problem, that her unwillingness to make love and lack of responsiveness mean she has a chronically low sex drive or even that she's "frigid." But Terri is not the ice queen she seems to be. She's simply a sexual Sleeping Beauty in dire need of a passionate wake-up kiss.

Terri used to enjoy making love—even at the end of a long day. But recently, she's allowed the rest of her life—a difficult job, a young child, and her commitment to a strict exercise regimen—to push her into a rut of sexual disinterest that has become increasingly difficult to climb out of. According to therapists, when a woman begins to feel annoyance rather than anticipation at the thought of sex, she mentally conditions herself to avoid arousal, *perpetuating* her apathy. Stretched and stressed to the max by each day's demands, Terri has sublimated her sexual desire until her libido has gone into complete hibernation—a natural response, but a destructive one.

In fact, a full and satisfying sex life is just the stress reducer Terri needs. Making love could *energize* rather than exhaust her, fill her with new self-esteem and confidence that she could use in her career and even at the gym. But point this out and she's likely to shake her head in frustration and say: "And just where am I supposed to fit it in? I'm overloaded as it is."

If this would be your answer as well—or there's any other reason your sex drive seems to have drifted into a deep snooze—you're not alone. In fact, what sex therapists have dubbed ISD (Inhibited Sexual Desire) is the number one sexual complaint in the U.S. today.

How could this happen in such a sex-obsessed

THE NICE GIRL'S GUIDE TO SENSATIONAL SEX

society, where erotic images ooze from every magazine page and television screen? Well, for many of us, sex just isn't fun anymore. We've let routine replace passion. Instead of doing "the wild thing," we feel we're doing the *boring* thing—and most of us would rather be doing something else.

In addition, many "nice girls" (and guys) who do try to blast away their bedroom boredom with something new find their choices limited by their own sexual belief system. They've been spoon-fed certain sexual myths since adolescence (some even earlier) and those half-truths and non-truths are still running—and sometimes ruining—their sex lives.

8 Myths That Can Stifle Your Sex Life

MYTH #1: IF HE LOVES ME, HE SHOULD KNOW HOW TO TURN ME ON

Bonnie was worried. Dean was the right man for her in every way but one—he was a major bumbler in bed. Just when she wanted him to speed up, he'd slow down. And when she needed a firm stroke, he'd touch her so lightly it tickled. She had hoped their lovemaking would improve, but now that they've been sleeping together for the last six months, she can no longer shake her doubts. "If he *were* the right man for me, wouldn't he know how to turn me on?" she asks her best friend. "I don't want to spend the rest of my life with a lousy lover. Maybe we're just not sexually compatible. Do you think I should break up with him?"

If she does, Bonnie is making a big mistake. It's true that Bonnie and Dean have a sexual problem, but its cause is not his lack of technique, but *her* lack of communication. Even though she's miserable, it would never occur to Bonnie to ask Dean to alter his touch or speed up his movements so that she could climax more easily. Instead, she expects him to read her mind and body and come to the correct conclusions on his own.

Bonnie has bought into the same myth that has wreaked havoc with many a potentially powerful sexual relationship. *Every* woman is so sexually unique, it's nearly impossible to know what really pleases her—unless she tells her lover in words or actions. To make matters more difficult for poor Dean, Bonnie's pleasure points, like those of many women, change according to where she is in her menstrual cycle. So just when he thinks he's found her hot spot, it turns out to have cooled.

But with just a bit of pillow talk Bonnie and Dean could synchronize their sexual styles and *save* their relationship. Therapists agree that communication is key to a good sexual (and otherwise) relationship, and it's a key Bonnie will have to learn to turn—before it's too late.

Myth #2: If You Love Someone, You Should Be Turned On By Him

Yes, you should—but not necessarily all the time or enough to experience an orgasm. If you're positively *revolted* by the prospect of having sex with a man you love, something is wrong, and you may need a few sessions with a therapist to work it out. But if the sex is simply less than spectacular, give yourself—and the guy—a chance. You're probably not doing anything wrong; it's just that you're not doing enough things right. Chances are, you simply need to explore and experiment until you find something that excites you.

Myth #3: Sex Should Be Spontaneous

From the moment Jeannie and Ron met during their first year of law school, their attraction was so intense they could hardly concentrate on their studies. They sometimes missed class to stay in bed together and made love in an empty classroom when they should have been hitting the books. Somehow they managed to pull in good grades anyway and have since both become winning trial lawyers working for rival firms.

But as their careers have skyrocketed, their sex life has taken a plunge. Constantly preparing cases or in court, they've gotten into the habit of making love only once a week on Friday nights. The sex itself is still terrific, but it isn't enough. They discussed the problem one Friday night, and Ron pulled out his date book. "I'm free next Wednesday from noon 'til two. Why don't we make an appointment with each other and get a motel room?"

But Jeannie balked, insisting, "That's so unromantic. Sex should be spontaneous. If you schedule it, it's not the same thing."

That's where Jeannie is wrong. Nostalgic for the "anytime, anywhere" sex of her student days, she's refusing to be realistic. With their booming law practices, it's unlikely either one of them will become less busy. So like many modern couples, Jeannie and Ron are going to have to be more flexible—and creative—if they want to combine career success and sex. Their scheduled tryst will increase their lovemaking frequency by 100 percent and there's no reason it can't be every bit as passionate as sex in an empty lecture hall once was.

Planning for their little orgy will only add to the pleasure. Jeannie could order a new silk teddy and g-string to give Ron a jolt (cotton panties are more her usual style). And Ron could catch her off-guard by making sure chilled champagne and candles are waiting for them in their room. If she'll give it a try, Jeannie may discover that *anticipation* can easily replace spontaneity as an equally powerful aphrodisiac.

MYTH #4: FANTASIZING DURING SEX IS CHEATING

Caitlin was horrified when she caught herself fantasizing about another man during intercourse with her boyfriend. She was attracted to the plumber with the tight buns who was fixing her sink. But while she had flirted with him and mused what it might be like to give him a little squeeze, she never expected a vision of those buns and the rest of his muscular body to pop up while she was in bed with her boyfriend. In fact, Caitlin was so upset with her "dirty" daydreaming that she switched off sexually and didn't climax as she usually did. "I felt like I was suddenly cheating on my boyfriend," she explains.

Of course, nothing could be further from the truth. She had never spoken more than a few sentences to her fantasy man, and she was in her boyfriend's arms, not his. Perhaps Caitlin would be comforted to know that studies have shown that up to 94 percent of women fantasize and that therapists insist that it's not only normal—it's *necessary*.

Fantasies trigger and maintain arousal so that

you can stop worrying about the presentation you have to give in the morning or the laundry that remains undone and simply concentrate on pleasure. And, as long as fantasizing about another lover isn't the *only* way you can respond to your mate, such musings provide a safe outlet for every woman's *natural* erotic curiosity about other men.

MYTH #5: MASTURBATION IS WRONG, ESPECIALLY IF YOU HAVE A HUSBAND OR LOVER

There's an old saying: half of all men admit they masturbate, and the other half are liars. By the time they reach adulthood, most men have accepted masturbation as a perfectly normal way to achieve sexual release, and indulge themselves without guilt. But many women, including some who consider themselves highly sexed, still seem to believe that there's something slightly depraved about pleasuring yourself.

If Sharon, 27, felt the urge to have sex and her lover, Howard, wasn't around, she would simply stifle her sexual needs until their next date. "I thought there was something shameful about wanting to touch myself," she explains, "so I just wouldn't—no matter what. But then Howard went on a business trip and we didn't see each other for a whole week. I was preparing a special, sexy welcome home and I started thinking about how wonderful it would feel to be back in bed with him, the delicious way he smelled, how his hands would feel on my body. I became so aroused I just couldn't stand it—and his plane wasn't due for hours!

"So I gave in and masturbated and it was like all the erotic energy I had been suppressing just exploded. I had an orgy with myself and Howard can home early and found me spread-legged on the bed. I had been afraid that masturbation would ruin my desire for intercourse, but was I wrong. The sex we had that night was the best ever. And Howard said that knowing I had 'prepared' myself for him really set him on fire, which made me feel a little less embarrassed about being caught that way."

Leslie also found masturbation distasteful—until she tried it out of necessity. Unlike Sharon, Leslie had no problem keeping her sexual urges in check. In fact, they seemed to be chained up somewhere deep inside her, with little hope for release. She hadn't climaxed for so long, she didn't even know if she still could.

Her lack of sexual response never really bothered Leslie until she met Dave, a man who stirred her emotionally like none had done before. "I wanted to go to bed with him to express my love, but my body just wouldn't cooperate. And the more I willed myself to have an orgasm, the further I got from having one.

"Finally, Dave asked me what was wrong, and I burst into tears. He comforted me and said he didn't want to pressure me. But I didn't want to lose him, so I was determined to make the next time better."

But how? Leslie was at a loss until a girlfriend suggested doing masturbation exercises (like the ones found in Chapter Two of this book) to discover what brought her to climax most easily. Once she found out, Leslie's friend advised, she'd be able to pass the information along to Dave.

At first, Leslie was shocked. But she was also desperate, so she took her friend's advice. It took several tries for her to break past the "Keep Out" sign she had posted in front of her sexuality, but once she did and saw she was still capable of climaxing, she was able to replace it with a new one that said, "Come and Get It!"

Myth #6: Sex With The Same Person Can't Stay Hot

Hope, a 28-year-old stock analyst, has been married for five years to Bruce, a banker, and has watched her sex life disintegrate from lusty all-night love sessions several times a week to a bland quickie every now and then. "I know that things are supposed to cool off after a while, but I'm starting to dread making love," she confides. "It doesn't do anything for me, and I'm beginning to feel this great distance between the two of us. I guess I just have the 'seven-year itch' two years early."

Hope and Bruce need to learn how to scratch that itch for one another before the sexual doldrums drag their marriage down further. Preventing the dwindling of desire *is* difficult in long-term relationships. According to one study, after four years, most couples typically have sex 25 percent less than they did when they first met. After twenty years, the frequency can drop to half that.

But just because your man becomes more familiar over time doesn't mean that sex has to become stale. "Sexual boredom is often due to laziness and the willingness to settle for 'pretty good,'" asserts Barbara DeAngelis, Ph.D., author of *Secrets About Men Every Woman Should Know*. But "happily, there is a way to break out of this cycle of passivity. *You* can take the lead. Show your eagerness. Seduce your husband. Become a more active partner in bed. When you do, you'll not only make him crazy for you again, you'll pave the way to sexier sex—for *both* of you."

MYTH #7: IT'S FINE TO FAKE IT

To fake or not to fake? It's a question that most woman have struggled with—usually with a well-meaning man pumping away above them and no possibility of orgasm below. "There are still women around who advocate faking orgasm, a practice stemming from the bad old days when the male ego was seen as more important than honest or mutual pleasure," says *Cosmopolitan*'s "Agony" columnist Irma Kurtz. "There are also women who derive immense enjoyment from lovemaking *without* achieving orgasm. They believe, with some justification, that no man is likely to understand how this could be possible; therefore, they fake orgasm." Whatever the reason, a whopping 66 percent of all women have faked orgasm at one time or another, according to the latest Kinsey Report.

But those women who fake orgasm consistently are ultimately cheating themselves and their lovers. Therapists agree that putting on an *occasional* performance isn't a real problem, especially if you're tired and don't think your partner will stop until you've climaxed. Faking can even be therapeutic. Some therapists even advise their clients to fake it until they make it—on the theory that acting out an orgasm may push past any "stage fright" a woman may have.

When a particular lovemaking session (with a new lover, perhaps) doesn't push you over the edge—and you don't feel like discussing it—pretending to climax is an option. But if it's your *only* option, you need to search for others. If your responses are always fake, there's a problem that has the potential to damage more than just your sexual relationship.

As Irma Kurtz points out, "Once the faking has begun, it is impossible to stop without not only distressing your partner, but also branding yourself a liar—and if you've lied to him about sex, he might think you've been untruthful about other things too."

So what's a girl to do? Don't blab your little secret, but *do* practice and experiment with giving yourself an orgasm so that faking it during lovemaking will no longer be necessary. You'll discover exactly how in the next chapter. And for those times when you absolutely, positively cannot come, don't immediately act out a passionate climax worthy of a porn queen. Try explaining to your lover that you can still enjoy yourself without one. You may be surprised to find out that he's a lot less hung up on mandatory orgasms than you are.

Myth #8: The Sex Won't Be Any Good If You Don't Love Him

In fact, the sex might be fantastic—but probably just on a temporary basis. Should you continue an affair with someone you don't love, you may end up feeling unsatisfied in bed *and* out. I know, I know. Theoretically, a woman should be able to have great sex without any strings attached. But, unfortunately, few women can separate their emotions so completely from their sexuality (not as many men, of course, seem to suffer from this problem).

There may actually be a scientific reason women feel such a strong need to connect sex with love. Oxytocin, dubbed "the love hormone" by sex researchers, is released in response to *nonphysical* cues that arouse us, such as a partner whispering, "I love you." Both sexes produce oxytocin, but studies have shown that women manufacture much more of it because we require more to reach orgasm. As a result, researchers theorize women may physically need more *emotional* arousal than men in order to enjoy sex.

So why not accept this part of your sexual make-up? And if you do find yourself in bed with a man whose prowess is formidable, but his personality is not, enjoy the sex for what it is and end the affair before it sours.

Ready, Set, Sex!

According to a recent study, a startling 64 percent of couples feel their sex lives are a flop, and the myths above are *major* contributors to that malaise. But forget about those sorry souls. You're about to join the remaining 36 percent who have found sexual bliss and manage to hold onto it.

Of course, even if you only have sex once a month, you have no problem—as long as you and your partner are happy. But if your typical once a month or once a week seems meager, it's possible to increase your levels of desire and satisfaction *without* the help of anyone but your partner.

As you'll discover in this chapter, there are many surprisingly *simple* ways to step on the gas and rev up your erotic engine. And even if your sex life is already running smoothly, the following suggestions can help you shift it into high gear. All you need is a good attitude and a little ingenuity.

Could You Be More Sexual?

You like sex—when you get around to having it. But like many women, it may rank low on your priority list—somewhere above having lunch with your mother-in-law but below doing well at your job, being a good parent, even improving your tennis serve. As a result, it gets pushed to the back burner, and by the time you do find yourself in bed, you're too exhausted to enjoy it. And when lovemaking becomes a pain instead of a pleasure, lunch with your mother-in-law starts looking good.

It doesn't have to be that way. But in order to make sex a top pleasure, it also has to be a top priority—at least some of the time. And to do that, you have to bring it out of the bedroom and into the rest of your life. No, that doesn't mean making love on the kitchen table (although that could help spice things up!). But you can learn to tap into your natural sexuality whenever you feel the urge, rather than immediately shutting it down the way so many of us do.

The warm, alive, *enthusiastic* quality you project when your sexual switch is always on creates a natural charisma that can help you get a raise in a recession or win a client no one else has been able to catch (not to mention a firm commitment from a previously uncommittable man). That's because when it comes right down to it, sex appeal really equals self-confidence, something everyone finds *extremely* appealing.

And if you already have that wonderful man and don't want to lose him, keeping him under your sexual spell will help prevent him from straying. Yes, in a perfect and politically correct world, you would be able to hold on to him simply by the power of your terrific personality. But, in reality, every couple needs some sexual cement to glue their relationship together. Making so-so sex into great sex can help you better tolerate each other's shortcomings and surmount the strain just living everyday life puts on most relationships.

Luckily, biology is on your side. Here's one fun fact I'll bet your high school sex education teacher never quite got around to telling you: the more you have sex, the more you will enjoy it—the chemicals in your brain guarantee it! If you start making love more often, the chemical communication between brain cells quickens and intensifies because the impulses are traveling on a well-beaten path. The payoff is an increase in pleasure *without* an increase in effort.

So, as if you hadn't guessed, the answer to the question at the beginning of this section is: yes, you could be more sexual—every woman can!

Break Down The Barriers

Many women erect walls around their sexuality by filling their lives with so many other activities and people that they have little, if any, time for making love. If that sounds familiar, take active steps to cut down on dinners with friends and Sundays with relatives and reserve the time for just the two of you. You don't have to use it to make love, but do spend it together—talking, walking, even playing a game of Monopoly. It will nurture the intimacy between you and, therefore, your sexual relationship.

Always projecting an "I'm too busy" attitude is another common brick wall some women build. Believe it or not, the sight of you working up a sweat as you ride your home exercise bike or an enticing view of your derriere as you bend over to load the dishwasher may be all it takes to arouse your lover. But many men won't act on these feelings because they're sure rejection is inevitable—and they're often right. As a result, the dishes may be clean, but yet another opportunity to make love—and strengthen the intimate bond between you—has been lost.

Other women unsuspectingly turn their bedroom into a bland neutral zone. It may be soothing to spend an hour reading in bed before sleep, but if you act *too* absorbed in your novel, that's all you'll ever get to do. And never, ever bring work to bed with you. There's nothing less sexy than a woman with a calculator in one hand and a spread sheet in the other who can't be interrupted until she finishes going over her figures.

When your man walks into the room, make it a point to smile and give him some of your attention. And if he wants to make love, at least open your mind to the possibility. Yes, the laundry may still need to be done or that report read for your meeting in the morning; but if you *always* put those tasks before sex, your priorities are mixed up. The truth is that if you're waiting for the perfect moment to make love, you may end up waiting yourself right out of a relationship.

Getting A Sexy Head Start

After you've broken down the barriers that were standing between you and better sex, you've got to learn how to actually bring sex out of the bedroom and into the rest of your life—and turn yourself into a totally sexual being. For example, most women throw cold water on the erotic musings that pop into their minds throughout the day because they are unable to act on them at the moment. But a totally sexual woman savors those sexy thoughts, allowing them to begin heating her up for a lovemaking session that may not take place until hours later.

Sex therapists have found that those women who climax most easily prime themselves for passion with erotic daydreaming throughout the day. By the time they actually come into contact with their lovers, many are able to reach orgasm simply by being touched on the earlobe, toe, or neck!

Okay, so maybe you'll never explode into ecstasy from a simple tug on your earlobe, but you *can* learn something from those lusty ladies. Start feeling sexual from the moment you wake up. Instead of jumping out of bed when the alarm clock rings, take a few minutes to cuddle with your lover. Better yet, set your alarm to go off a half-hour early—plenty of time for a passionate quickie with a lover, or by yourself.

Am I advocating early morning masturbation? You bet! An orgasm is an energizing, stress-reducing way to start the day, and there's no reason you should deprive yourself if you're currently unattached.

Keep the sensual spirit alive when you get out of bed by slipping on some silky lingerie instead of

THE NICE GIRL'S GUIDE TO SENSATIONAL SEX 17

your old cotton panties. If you have a partner, be sure to include him as well. Make getting dressed for work a performance he'll remember all day long. Point your toes prettily as you put on your panty hose. Then ask him to hook your bra and zip up your dress, dropping your hair over his hands before they leave your shoulders. Keep the top button of your blouse open until the last minute and request his aid in dabbing a bit of his favorite perfume deep into your cleavage.

And even if he doesn't ask for it, give him some hands-on pampering: straighten his tie, smooth his hair, even zip up his pants (slowly). If you have some extra time, take your morning shower together and make him wash your hair *before* he does anything else.

Even once you're out and about, you can still fuel the fire. Try these naughty techniques or make up your own:

- Turn your commute together into something more. Start the day off with a kiss at every stop light and keep your hand on his thigh.
- If your togetherness time is being whittled down by working out, exercise together at the health club or at home. Wear something skimpy and let him see your body glistening with sweat. Watch the way his muscles move as he lifts weights. You'll see that exercise can be an *extraordinary* sexual energizer.

Terri, who packed every minute of her life chock-full with everything *but* sex, reluctantly invited her husband Rich to the gym when he said he wanted to spend more time with her. Busy with her workout, she turned and caught sight of Rich, his biceps bulging as he pumped an impressive amount of iron, and was reminded of the days when he was the well-toned star of the high school track team and she couldn't wait to touch him after his practice.

That memory was powerful motivation. Terri cut her workout short, and ten minutes later she was making energetic love to Rich (and burning more calories than she usually did on the stairclimber).

- Make eye and hand contact across the dinner table. Pretend you're on a first date and want to impress him. Give him a look and a squeeze that tells him he's the most attractive man around and that he's captured *all* your attention.
- Be a tease. Absence definitely makes the heart (and other body parts) grow hotter. Abstain from sex for a few days, teasing your partner instead with light but lascivious kisses and "accidental" erotic touches. Hold him off gently, but firmly, until the two of you *must* have more.

REWRITE YOUR SEXUAL SCRIPT

Once you're in bed—or on the living room floor, the kitchen table, or even in the bathtub—refuse to let yourself fall into a pattern of making love the same old way every time. When you find something that works, you may be reluctant to abandon it for uncharted territory, but you must if you're to wake up your sleepy libido and expand your sexual horizons.

Here are a few foolproof ways to begin:

THE NICE GIRL'S GUIDE TO SENSATIONAL SEX 19

- Rent an X-rated video and let him "catch" you watching it alone. Then act out the starring role for him.
- Have a picnic in bed. Feed him his favorite finger foods, and offer yourself (topped with hot fudge, perhaps) as dessert.
- Plan an evening of erotic games: spin-the-bottle, strip poker, and fill-in-the-blanks (cross out the characters' names in a letter from *Penthouse* or a steamy passage from a trashy novel and substitute your lover's and your own. Then read aloud for hilarious and sexy results).
- Make out. If you haven't done it since high school, you're definitely missing a wonderful way to drive yourselves crazy with desire. To make your engines really purr, pick him up after work in a rented Porsche or another supersexy dream car (not too much money for just one day), race down the highway with the wind in your hair, and park somewhere special under the stars. Or find a secluded pair of seats in a movie theater's balcony and neck for *hours*. If you're doing it right, you'll never remember the film's plot.
- Bring home some sex toys and teach him how they work (more on this in Chapter Seven).
- Tie him to the bedposts and "torture" him with your tongue (see page 163 for for some crucial tips). Then switch positions.
- Try unusual locations. Make love on the living room rug, in a bubble bath by candlelight, on a blanket in the backyard, or on the beach after dark.
- Read a sex manual *together* and pick out a

new technique to try. Bonnie had branded her boyfriend Dean a sexual incompetent without ever giving him instructions on how to please her. All that changed when she brought a sex manual to bed one night. "I was too shy to actually come right out and ask, so I simply pointed to a position I wanted to try and Dean performed it," she says, delight and a little awe in her voice. "The man could be a professional! Now I can't wait to try a new technique every night."

- Greet him at the door naked (an oldie, but still a goodie!)

If, after you come to bed wearing a peek-a-boo bra instead of your usual flannel nightie and brandishing your new vibrator, your lover asks what's gotten into you, *do not* announce that you're bored with your sex life and you're trying to break the awful monotony (a definite desire damper). Just smile mysteriously and say you're feeling playful.

In addition, don't try out your whole bag of tricks at once. Just one or two a week will perk up his interest (and yours) and leave you with plenty of new erotic extras for next time.

And if the first few teasers you try fall flat, don't pout and give up. Employ another from the list or your own imagination. Keep an open—and creative—mind, and you'll discover many hidden opportunities for great sex almost *everywhere*.

2
IN SEARCH OF THE BIG "O"

Six months ago, Annie, 20, ended a two-year relationship with the man to whom she'd lost her virginity. Jordan was thirty-three and a very experienced lover. It seemed he always knew exactly where to touch her, and Annie had an orgasm almost every time they had sex. For the last month, Annie's been dating Mark, 22, and has fallen deeply in love with him. But their first night in bed—as well as every night since—was a disaster. Mark's lovemaking style is quicker and rougher than Jordan's, and Annie has stopped having orgasms. In fact, without the long, luscious foreplay she had come to depend on, Annie has stopped enjoying sex altogether. But she hasn't told Mark what she _would_ enjoy for fear of wounding his ego. So Annie continues to suffer in silence, dreading each night they spend together.

Mandy, 28, has been happily married—and happily faking orgasm—for six years. At least, she _thought_ she was happy until one of her girlfriends began talking about a new lover and the marvelous climaxes they had reached together. Then another pal chimed in with her tales of erotic ecstasy, and Mandy began to realize how much she had been missing. She had always found sex pleasant, but never more. After the first few lovemaking sessions with her husband had failed to produce even a tiny *orgasm for her during intercourse, she'd stopped trying and started to act out Academy Award-winning climaxes. Whenever she needed an orgasm, she turned to masturbation, and found one every time. It had always seemed the easiest—and most ego-sparing—way to go, but now she wasn't so sure. When she heard her friends brag about the fun they were having in bed, she felt left out—and confused. Still, what could she possibly do to change a sexual pattern that had been in place for years?*

Sara, 31, isn't sure if she's <u>ever</u> had an orgasm. She's certainly never felt the sort of limb-thrashing, teeth-gnashing climaxes she's seen women experience in movies. The most she's experienced is a sort of general warmth in her groin and a few mild flutters. Morally opposed to the notion of faking, Sara has drifted from lover to lover, always hoping her response will be different, that the next man will be the one to breathe life into her sexuality and give her the sort of explosive orgasms she dreams about. But all she ever feels are those frustrating flutters, and she blames the fact that she's still single on her "frigidity."

Like Annie, Mandy, and Sara, millions of women have trouble experiencing orgasm with their partners—or even by their own hands. According to *The Kinsey Institute New Report on Sex*, fewer than 50 percent of all women are able to reach orgasm through intercourse when the only form of stimulation is a thrusting penis, and 10 percent never reach orgasm at all. Yet most of those millions ignore their problem, accepting it passively even though it makes them deeply unhappy.

These women feel they're missing something—and they're right. They're completely comfortable

THE NICE GIRL'S GUIDE TO SENSATIONAL SEX 23

telling their husbands or lovers to do the dishes or have dinner with their parents, but making a sexual request is out of the question. As a result, they feel sexually unsatisfied and are unable to achieve the ultimate relationship goal of most women: true and total intimacy with their partners.

The reasons are obvious. Even those who are completely happy with their sex lives are still a little ashamed of being sexual because of all the negative messages they've received from their parents, their religion, and society at large. In addition, some may have suffered sexual, physical, or emotional abuse that makes it impossible for them to enjoy themselves sexually, and they may need psychological therapy before they can approach lovemaking happily.

But the *majority* of women can break past those barriers of guilt and shame and solve their orgasm problems on their own. If you're one of them, you should know that the power to experience thrillingly satisfying climaxes has always been within you, and this chapter will show you exactly how to unleash your orgasmic potential or increase what you already have. And learning these techniques is a lot easier—and more pleasurable—than you might think.

If you rely on your partner to provide you with an orgasm, you might not get one. But once you know exactly what you need and how to achieve it (with a partner or without), you'll never have to wonder what all that talk of "exquisite agony" is about, you'll *know!*

Our lesson begins with what an orgasm is and *can* be. Next, you'll learn how to discover the best way to achieve orgasm *for you* through a series of sensual sexercises. Then, I'll reveal how to gild that gorgeous lily with *lots* of extras to enhance your entire sexual experience.

There are only three requirements. The first two are an open mind and a sincere desire to increase your orgasmic potential. You've proven you have the first by picking up this book. You may think you have the second until you come to the first sexercise and begin to feel a little self-conscious about actually doing it or afraid that nothing will happen and you'll feel like a failure. You may even be tempted to skip around until you come to a technique that you feel confident you *will* get results from. But if you do that, you'll simply be teaching yourself what you already know.

Instead, put aside your doubts and dive in with only one purpose: to see what you can learn about your sexual self. If that's your goal, there's no way you can fail. Make a commitment to try each of the sexercises at least five times. Nothing much may happen the first time, but that doesn't mean you won't feel fireworks the second or third. In fact, you may find these sexercises so effective, you'll want to make them a regular part of your sexual repertoire. Believe me, the rewards—delicious, stress-reducing, satisfying, almost addictive orgasms—are worth the effort. Besides, practicing will be fun!

The final requirement is time, something most of us have all too little of. Still, if you're not willing to set aside one private, uninterrupted hour or so a few days a week to give the sexercises in this chapter a chance to work, you might as well stop reading now.

Annie, whom you met at the beginning of this chapter, is a full-time graduate student and part-time salesclerk in a bookstore, and was sure she'd never be able to capture that much free time. The real problem was not her school work or her job, but the fact that she hadn't yet made sex a priority in her life—and until she did, she was not likely to start enjoying it more with her new lover.

Like many women, Annie was willing to spend hours searching the stores for the perfect dress to wear to a party, but unwilling to make the time to go on a much more productive sexual search. One reason was that she believed that if she and her partner were truly in love, having great sex with him should come naturally and spontaneously. This had been true with Jordan, but she was finding out with Mark that this was not always going to be the case. Still, she felt that there was something wrong with practicing sexual techniques—or even telling her lover to lighten his touch here, and press a little harder there. As a result, when Annie and Mark didn't achieve perfect sexual sync after several lovemaking sessions, she began to doubt their whole relationship—in bed and out.

As any sex therapist will tell you, the romantic, idealized image of lovemaking that Annie holds so dear is a myth, and a dangerous one at that. It's kept many women (and men) from feeling free to hone the skills that would make sex much more pleasurable for themselves and their partners. The truth is that great lovemaking almost always requires great trust in your partner and a detailed knowledge of what turns him or her on—both of which take time to achieve, time during which the sex you do have may be less than spectacular.

In addition, sexual skills have to be learned and practiced like any others. Few people are born fantastic lovers. The rest of us have to work at it, but, at least, it's some of the most enjoyable work you'll ever do!

So, if you've been making excuses when you should be making time to practice, why not get out your date book and schedule a sexual appointment with yourself? And don't break it!

Finally, even if you've never had trouble reaching orgasm by yourself or with a partner, read on. The information and sexercises that follow will broaden your orgasmic horizons and inject more variety into your sex life. You may discover something—a new way to stroke, a different position—you never knew felt good before. You have nothing to lose but your sexual limitations.

Anatomy Of An Orgasm

Before you begin your experiment with ecstasy, it's important to know a little bit about your own anatomy and that of an orgasm. If you've never taken a really good look at your vagina, join the club! While many women know the exact measurement of their waists, the contours of their hips, and every pore on their faces, few have ever investigated what they actually look like "down there."

So go ahead and take a peek—no one's watching. Lie down and use a hand mirror or, better still, a makeup mirror that stands on its own. You may need to use pillows to prop yourself up at the right angle. Yes, it does look a little strange at first. It may even seem ugly to you, but rest assured that few men would agree. (So, when you're in bed later with a lover who wants to slide down to investigate, don't be shy. The look, smell, and taste of you will only arouse him further.)

Like no two faces, no two vaginas are exactly

THE NICE GIRL'S GUIDE TO SENSATIONAL SEX

alike. Compared to a picture in a biology textbook, your outer lips may be longer, your clitoris may be bigger or smaller (size doesn't affect sexual pleasure), or the head of the clitoris might be hidden entirely by its hood and impossible to see.

It's a trendy thing these days to know your sex organs inside and out. One famous sex therapist, Lonnie Barbach, even suggests *drawing* your vagina to help you concentrate on how all its different little parts fit together. I don't think you have to go that far, but if you're trying to increase your orgasmic potential, it does pay to be familiar with the territory.

The same goes for orgasms. How do you know if you're headed for this state of ultimate bliss? When your partner, your vibrator, or even a trashy novel turns the sexual heat up high, your entire body may become almost rigid with sexual tension (some women misinterpret this as anxiety and shut down their response, making it difficult, even impossible to achieve orgasm). In addition, your pelvic area may begin to do an involuntary dance of pleasure, moving up and down, back and forth, or in circular motion. And you'll probably start breathing heavily, perhaps panting, sighing, and moaning.

At the same time, blood will start flowing into your vagina, swelling the clitoris, the outer and inner lips, and the general pelvic area. Your nipples may also swell and other parts of your body tingle and ache to be touched.

All this swelling causes the vagina to lubricate so a penis can slide in and out easily. But keep in mind that just as being "wet" doesn't mean you're ready to have intercourse, you can feel *very* ready and not be wet at all. After Mandy gave birth to her daughter, who is now two years old, she began to feel her body had betrayed her. Not only did her vagina feel looser, it seemed to stubbornly refuse to lubricate—even when she was dying to have sex. As a result, she endured many painful episodes of intercourse until a friend suggested dabbing on a bit of lubricant. Now she keeps a tube stashed in her night table. (If you use a lubricant, make sure it's water-based. See page 199 for a list of some good brands).

Finally, right before orgasm, the PC (pubococcygeal) muscle that surrounds the entrance of the vagina will also swell, and may cause that opening to tighten, making it slightly difficult for a penis that's not already inside to get past. This makes many women worry that they're not turned on enough to have sex when, in fact, the complete opposite is true. At this point the clitoris usually retracts under its hood and the ever-elusive G-spot (see page 53) also swells and becomes more sensitive.

With continued stimulation, the tension, swelling, and lubricating continue until your body reaches its peak and you have an orgasm, which, for all the hoopla surrounding it, is simply a reversal of the process just described. The blood that's been swelling everything like crazy is suddenly released and flows back to the rest of the body, the uterus or pelvic muscles may contract several times (many women have these contractions but don't feel them), and the tension that tightened every muscle so marvelously suddenly relaxes as well.

Some women are completely satisfied and "spent" by one orgasm, while others remain aroused and want more. A recent survey found that 48 percent of all women are *multi*orgasmic. And according to Dr. Kenneth Davidson of the University of Wisconsin, who conducted the survey, "Every woman is physically capable of having multiple orgasms. After an orgasm, a woman relaxes but [unlike a man's penis] her clitoris stays erect. She stays aroused much longer than her partner."

In addition, sex researchers have made the startling discovery that women can ejaculate (yes, you read it right!) during orgasm. Some women fear that the little spurt of clear liquid is urine, and so try to hold it back (they end up holding back their orgasms as well). In fact, research shows that the fluid (usually just a teaspoon or so) comes from glands and ducts that surround the G-spot inside your vagina, and is a sign of *intense* arousal.

Your Kind Of Climax

Most experts now agree that there are at least two general types of orgasms—clitoral and vaginal—that follow similar physical patterns but feel very different because they seem to originate in different spots. How can you tell what type of orgasm you've had? A clitoral climax generally feels like a short, sharp pang of pleasure concentrated in the clitoris. On the other hand, a vaginal orgasm, which seems to be triggered by a penis stimulating the entrance to your vagina and/or thrusting against your G-spot, is usually felt as a more widespread meltdown.

As one woman described it, "When I masturbate, I concentrate on my clitoris and the climaxes I have feel like intense bursts of pleasure centered right there. During intercourse, however, my clitoris gets only indirect stimulation. It takes me longer to come, and when I do, it feels more like soft waves of pleasure that radiate through my entire body. But if I or my partner gently rubs my clitoris by hand while he's inside me, sometimes I can feel it *everywhere* when I climax, in my clitoris and the rest of my body at the same time—and those orgasms are really wonderful."

Whether clitoral or vaginal, orgasms vary enormously in duration and sensation from woman to woman, and from one sexual encounter to the next. Every woman's response is so unique, in fact, that sex therapists coined the phrase "orgasmic fingerprinting" to emphasize its individuality. Just how hot you become during any particular lovemaking session depends on your personal sexual history and anatomy, how much you like or love your partner, the length of foreplay, your self-esteem at the moment, and, of course, good ol' hormones.

Another major factor is your expectations—expectations that have probably been heavily influenced by society, and not always in a beneficial way. Freud, the father of psychoanalysis and, some would say, of many of today's female sexual problems, believed that clitoral orgasms were okay for adolescents, but that any "mature" woman should have progressed to having vaginal orgasms, which only a man's penis could provide. If not, he concluded, that poor woman needed years of therapy.

A fine theory—except that female sexuality just doesn't work like that. In fact, among the women Shere Hite polled for *The Hite Report*, 70 percent said they needed clitoral stimulation for orgasm, which occurs only *indirectly* (if at all) during intercourse in the missionary position so beloved by

THE NICE GIRL'S GUIDE TO SENSATIONAL SEX 31

most men. Unfortunately, because of the wide acceptance of Freud's general theory that the only "correct" orgasm is one that comes from a man's penis, many women who can't come this way have been labeled—or labeled themselves—frigid. This was certainly true in Sara's case. Caught up in the assumption that the only way to climax acceptably was through intercourse, she had never tried any other way—and was unable to get the clitoral stimulation she didn't even know she desperately needed.

As sex educator Betty Dodson points out in her book *Sex for One: The Joy of Selfloving*, "Frigid is a man's word for a woman who can't have an orgasm in the missionary position in a few minutes with only the kind of stimulation that's good for him. The truth is, very few women consistently reach orgasm in intercourse without additional stimulation. Imagine a man trying to have an orgasm without touching the head of his penis." So there's no need to be worried or depressed if the same is true for you.

The Principles Of Self-Pleasure

Before you can tell or show your partner how to help you have an orgasm—or how to improve the orgasms you've been having—you have to learn yourself. And the best way to do that is through masturbation. According to the latest statistics from the Kinsey Institute report, between 60 and 80 percent of all women have masturbated at some point in their lives. However, many—especially those who have had steady sex partners—have not done so on a regular basis since they were teenagers. As a result, they may be missing out on an effective way they can gather important sexual information about themselves, information that will ultimately improve sex *with* their partners.

"Know thyself" is perhaps the most important rule when it comes to achieving or improving orgasms. If you're ignorant of your own pleasure preferences, you won't be able to communicate them to your partner. And no matter how much your lover wants to please you, his efforts will be hit or miss at best—a situation more likely to lead to frustration than sexual bliss.

But if you take the time to learn your body's preferences and rhythms through masturbation, you'll be able to pass them along to your man through words or touch. And believe me, he'll be grateful. Most men desperately want to please their partners—in fact, their sexual egos depend on it. If you let him know how he can get results, it will allow *both* of you to relax and enjoy yourselves more.

That's where masturbation comes in. "What better way to learn about pleasure and being sexually creative? We don't have to perform or meet anyone else's standards, to satisfy the needs of a partner, or to fear criticism or rejection for failure," explains Dodson, who was dubbed the "Mother of Masturbation" after she published her manual on the art of self-pleasure and began to give how-to workshops. "Sexual skills are like any other skills; they're not magically inherited, they have to be learned."

Masturbation is an excellent teacher. If we learn its lessons, Dodson believes, "When we're asked what feels good, we will have the courage to let go of our little white lie, 'Oh everything you do feels good.'" Discovering how to pleasure yourself is also the short road to orgasm for women like Sara who have never had one before. As sex therapists have discovered, every woman is physically capable of having an orgasm—if she gets the clitoral stimulation she needs. Since such stimulation is limited in intercourse but *un*limited in masturbation, the latter is the way to open up your orgasmic potential.

Many women feel "funny" about practicing this particular skill, having been taught from childhood that masturbation is wrong, and that it can even cause psychological or physical problems. Annie hadn't masturbated since she was caught by her mother when she was eight and was told her vagina would close up if she continued to play with herself. By the time she realized that was only a cruel fairy tale, its moral had already taken hold in her mind.

Sara also hadn't masturbated she since was a child because she had read somewhere that she could become hooked on self-pleasuring and would never want to have sex with a man. Adamantly anti-drug and all things addictive, Sara refused to give in to the temptation to touch herself. But like the tale Annie's mother told, Sara's fears couldn't be further from the truth. Numerous masturbation studies have been done the world over, and all have concluded that masturbation is a wonderful way to relieve sexual stress and only *increases* a woman's desire for partner sex.

But there's another *essential* reason for giving it a try. Masturbation is empowering. According to Drs. Julia Heiman and Joseph LoPiccolo, the authors of *Becoming Orgasmic*, "It emphasizes a very important and very basic fact: *Your body belongs first of all to you.* Unless you can develop some kind of sense that your body is *your* territory (which you can choose to give as a gift, share, or keep to yourself), you cannot freely give it in a sexual interaction with another person. It will seem that the other person already owns it, and when that occurs you are less likely to feel you have the right to say yes or no to sex, less likely to help guide the sexual interaction, less likely to try sexual activities that interest you, and even less likely to know what you want sexually."

That said, there's no reason you have to make masturbation a habit, although many women do. (One friend, who has no lack of lovers, masturbates regularly. She calls it "the perfect tranquilizer" and relies on it to relax her whenever she has trouble sleeping.) But try to put aside your concerns at least long enough to learn what you can from the following sexercise, which will enrich your sex life whether or not you climax easily. Then you never have to do it again (although I hope you'll want to).

Sexercise One: Erotic Self-Exploration

Read the entire sexercise *before* you begin. Once you embark on your erotic adventure, you don't want to have to drag yourself down by carefully going over the instructions. Your first time out, don't skip a step, even if it seems silly. Next time, you can choose the steps that work for you and discard those that don't, but give each process a chance to work its magic this time around. In addition, allow yourself at least an hour of private time, preferably in the early evening.

THE NICE GIRL'S GUIDE TO SENSATIONAL SEX

Part One

1. The idea behind this first step is to relax and start thinking sexually, even if you've had a terrible day. Few people can stay tense in a hot bath, so run one for yourself and throw in some bubble bath or bath oil to make the water feel silky. Blow up a bath pillow if you have one or roll up a towel to cradle your head. If possible, turn off the lights and illuminate the room with several candles instead. You can play some music, but make sure it's not too distracting. Have a glass of wine waiting tubside or a piece of chocolate (a substance known to encourage the release of endorphins, your brain's own pleasure-enhancing chemicals). And make sure you have something titillating to read.

2. Slip into the warm water and stretch out. Close your eyes and clear your thoughts. Your goal is *not* to have an orgasm, but to learn how you like to be touched when you're first becoming aroused so that you can eventually share that information with your lover. But don't worry about him now. Be completely selfish and think only of yourself. Let the water caress your body and loosen your muscles as you perform this classic, easy relaxation technique. Breathe deeply, and beginning with your toes, tense each part of your body, hold the tension for three seconds, and relax. Move on to your calves, your thighs, your buttocks, and so on, up your body until you run out of things to tense. This should leave you feeling soft and flexible. If not, try repeating this step.

3. Open your eyes and pick up whatever you've chosen to read. It can be anything, but it must be *sexy*, and the more stimulating, the better. If you find magazines like *Penthouse* or *Playgirl* too raunchy, you could try one of Nancy Friday's books of women's sexual fantasies (*My Secret Garden* or *Forbidden Flowers*) or even the steamier passages of a Judith Krantz novel.

   As you read and sip wine or nibble chocolate, you'll probably start feeling sexy. (Although if you don't, it's okay. Keep reading or try playing a favorite sex fantasy in your mind.) When you feel aroused, begin to touch your body tenderly, but avoid your breasts and vagina for the moment. It's best if you put your book down at this point and try to tune in to what you're feeling. Continue thinking sexy thoughts, perhaps spinning out something you've just read into a fantasy. Close your eyes and let your fingers slide over your body, focusing on which parts tingle and which don't. Massage the areas that respond most again and again, concentrating on how it feels to be touched there, whether you like a gentle squeeze or a hard stroke, whether you like a slow tempo or a staccato beat. Don't forget the back of your neck, your hairline, your hands, your earlobes, your calves, buttocks, even your toes. All are potential erogenous zones.

4. Now move on to your breasts and vagina. Alternate firm and soft strokes, slow and fast ones. Try fondling your nipples gently, then giving them a little pinch. *Remember, your goal is to teach yourself what feels good—*

THE NICE GIRL'S GUIDE TO SENSATIONAL SEX 37

not to have an orgasm. If you do climax, enjoy it. But more important, you want to step out of that tub with a good idea of how you like to be touched *before* you get to that point. You'll be able to use that precious information later.

5. Step out of the bath and dry yourself off gently with a big fluffy towel. (If you're out of time, you can stop now, but it's best to continue with Part Two to get the full impact of the sexercise.) As you rub yourself with the towel, take a moment to remember what felt good and what didn't. When you're completely dry, lie down on your bed or a comfortable couch to continue.

PART TWO

The next part of this sexercise will help teach you what will and won't bring you to orgasm so that you can share this information with your lover—and so you can enjoy a rollicking good time whenever you're alone and feel like indulging yourself (with no fat or calories, an orgasm is the perfect treat!).

If I could tell you *the* best way to masturbate, I would make millions. I can't. But I can tell you how other women pleasure themselves and give you some helpful hints. Then you'll just have to experiment.

Although no two women bring themselves to climax in exactly the same way, many press down firmly on the pubic mound with one palm and rub the side of their clitoris (avoiding contact with the sometimes painfully sensitive head) with their fingers (perhaps lubricated with saliva, vaginal fluid, or some sort of lotion). They may massage up and down or in circles, on one side of the clitoris or both (switching sides if too much pressure causes numbness in one area), usually increasing the tempo as arousal builds. They may also slip one or two fingers inside the vagina, and move them around or in and out.

With the other hand, a woman may touch her breasts or other hot spots, or pull, rub, or press together the outer lips of her vagina. Unlike men, who usually stop thrusting at the moment of orgasm, most women continue their exquisite manipulations all the way through their climax.

There are thousands (maybe *millions*) of variations on this theme. Some women like to rhythmically press their pelvis against something firm like a pillow or piece of furniture in order to reach orgasm through pressure alone. Others rely on the rhythmic clenching and releasing of the perineal muscles surrounding the vagina and anus. Still others like to use the jets of water from a hand-held shower head. Some masturbate lying on their backs, other on their stomachs, and others get the biggest climatic kick standing in front of a mirror and watching themselves. As you can see, there are many options—different strokes for different folks.

If you haven't masturbated in a while (or ever), rest assured that it can be a lot stranger reading about it than doing it, which is Part Two of this sexercise.

1. Lying comfortably on your bed or a couch, run your hands over your body in slow motion. You can use some body lotion or oil, if you'd like (even vegetable oil feels nice!). If you're afraid of making a mess, put a towel

under you. As you did in Part One, try to tune in to what feels good and what doesn't. Call up a favorite fantasy, read some more erotic material, and follow the game outlined above or your own strategy. Don't think about trying to climax, but do concentrate on how you can bring your body the most pleasure—and make a real effort.
2. As you start to soar higher, tease yourself a little. And whenever you feel close to coming, slow down, prolonging the peak as much as possible. After you climax, relax and take a few minutes to relive the entire experience in your mind, from the very first touch. Think about what sorts of strokes and rhythms started you off on the road to arousal and which ones finally got you there. That way, you'll be able to repeat your performance and enhance sex with your partner with the same sort of stimulation.

If you're almost at orgasm and get stuck, here are a few hints from sexperts Heiman and LoPiccolo that can help push you over the cliff to climax.

- Deliberately tense your legs, stomach, arms, or feet to mimic or exaggerate sexual tension.
- Do some vaginal muscle contractions (Kegel exercises—see page 50) to increase arousal and focus on your genital sensations.
- Change position so that your head hangs over the edge of the bed (this increases blood flow to your brain and changes your breathing, both of which can add to arousal).
- Try teasing yourself unmercifully, the way a

good lover would do. Move away from the area you've been concentrating on, only to return with light flicks and barely there strokes until your body absolutely *aches* to be touched.
- Call a time out and read a favorite passage from an erotic book or try imagining yourself in your most *intense* fantasy.
- Try a different position. Turn over on your stomach or your side, pull your knees up, or stretch out.
- If you've been lying still, move your hips in sync with your hands, even if it feels a bit forced at first.
- Hold your breath for a short time, then pant heavily.

Once Annie, who had never masturbated to orgasm as an adult, got over her initial resistance to the idea, she was delighted with the results of this sexercise. Particularly slow to arouse (hence her problems with her new lover Mark, who likes his lovemaking quick and rough), she discovered exactly which types of caresses would bring her to the boiling point most quickly.

Mandy, who had honed faking orgasm with her husband into a fine art, already masturbated frequently to get the satisfaction she was missing in the rest of her sex life. But she had never thought much about what she was doing to herself that her husband was not. For her, this sexercise illuminated the drastic differences—differences that she will still have to communicate to him if she wants her situation to improve.

It took several sessions for Sara to respond. But once she did, she felt as though she had finally found the "on" switch to her sexuality. Far from frigid, she discovered she was capable of tremendous erotic explosions and could hardly wait to try her new expertise out on a partner.

If you've *never* had an orgasm, it may take several attempts (or more) before you're able to discover exactly what works for your body, so don't get discouraged. This is one case where practice will definitely make perfect!

A Little Technology

Sara owes part of her success to her willingness to try the technological approach to orgasm. You may never have considered using a vibrator. It may seem too mechanical or unnatural. But for many women, it could mean the difference between having tiny or huge orgasms—or having any orgasms at all. "During intercourse, the penis pushes and pulls against the labia and clitoris and, so to speak, flicks on millions of tiny switches which fire off electric impulses to the brain," explains Dr. Miriam Stoppard in her book *The Magic of Sex*. "In a given moment a vibrator can trigger at least a million more sensors than the most educated penis, and that means orgasm is virtually inevitable." So don't turn up your nose at the mechanical approach yet!

There are many women who can't learn how to have a first orgasm by intercourse or manual masturbation and may need a vibrator to show them the way. In addition, "A vibrator can tear down the barriers of guilt, shame, and prudery that prevent so many women from finding the sexual fulfillment that they deserve," argues Stoppard. "Some women have for years subconsciously imposed the same kind of paralysis on their sex organs as on their minds. An electric vibrator provides intense, almost unbearable sexual excitement, sufficient to overwhelm emotional obstacles, and makes the brain and the genital organs respond explosively in unison." Other women, who are already orgasmic, just love the incredible sensations electric stimulation provides.

Even with a vibrator, a woman may need a long time to reach climax, sometimes as much as forty-five minutes or *more*. But many discover, to their delight, that a vibrator sends them hurtling towards orgasm in as little as sixty seconds.

That quickness was the key to Sara's first "I can really feel it" orgasm in years. After trying the preceding sexercises twice, she had felt a few flutters, but not much more, and she was disappointed and frustrated. That's when a friend, whom she had confided in, suggested a little mechanical help. "At first, I balked," Sara admits. "It seemed like such a cold-blooded approach. But I was beginning to feel bad about myself and my inability to reach orgasm. So when my friend told me that she owned a vibrator and it *always* worked, I figured it was worth a shot."

And what a shot it was! "I was lying in bed with the lights off and the vibrator in my hand. With a lot of skepticism, I turned it on and put it on the outside of my vagina, on my pubic mound, because the thing was big and buzzing and I was too afraid to touch my clitoris with it," Sara explains. "At first, I just felt those flutters again. But then, all of a sudden, this incredible sensation kicked in. Before I knew what I was doing, I felt this tremendous need to press the vibrator down hard on my vagina, and—pow!—this sharp jolt of pleasure hit

THE NICE GIRL'S GUIDE TO SENSATIONAL SEX

me. I knew that was a real orgasm, and I had five more the same way that night!"

VIBRATOR DOS AND DON'TS

Once you have your vibrator in your hands, you'll have to experiment to see what feels best. Like Sara, many women feel most comfortable keeping their vibrator on the *outside* of their vaginas, and either press it or rotate it on their pubic mound. For some, the stimulation may still be too intense in this position. In that case, placing a towel between you and your machine (or keeping your underwear on) will create a helpful buffer. If your machine features only one or two speeds and you want to have more precise control, Joani Blank, the author of *Good Vibrations: The Complete Guide to Vibrators* (yes, there's actually a whole book on the subject!), suggests attaching a conventional (rheostat) light dimmer to regulate it. (But never lower the speed so much that you can hear the machine struggle or you may burn out the motor.)

Or, you may want all the speed money can buy and find that placing the vibrator directly on the shaft of your clitoris finally provides you with the intense, focused stimulation you've been searching for. The only way to figure out what feels good for you is to play with your new toy and pay close attention to the sensations.

Start off slow on a low speed and use a light hand, increasing pressure and perhaps the speed as your arousal builds. One important note: a vibrator can create focused pleasurable sensations so intense they may feel almost painful at first. In fact, many women do misinterpret these feelings as pain and move the machine to another spot or stop using it altogether. But, if this happens to you, try to keep going for a moment. Often, this "pain" quickly blossoms into the pleasurable beginnings of an orgasm.

If you continue to feel uncomfortable or sore after a few moments, however, move the vibrator on to another area. And, if any part of your vagina should become numb (usually the result of pressing the machine on one "good" spot for a long time), pausing for a few minutes will return your feeling to normal.

Whatever method you choose, give your mighty little machine a chance to work. "When a woman is new to vibrator sex, she may experience any number of responses," Betty Dodson explains in her masturbation manual *Sex for One: The Joy of Selfloving*. "One friend reported that the first time she used her vibrator, she had the most intense orgasm of her life, but it was over before she knew what had happened. Another said her orgasm was ever so slight, lasting only a second. And yet another woman had to practice patiently for several months before anything sexual happened."

If your response is less than you expected, you may be experiencing a purely technical difficulty. The cause is usually not enough pressure—or too much. Too little will fail to increase the blood circulation which helps cause sexual arousal. So the solution may be as simple as taking away the towel you've been using between you and the vibrator or turning up the speed. Or you may be pressing down too hard directly on your clitoris and irritating it too much to experience any pleasure. If that's the case, try placing your vibrator a little to the left or right, lowering the speed, and using a lighter hand.

Or you may be experiencing what Dell Williams, the president of Eve's Garden, a wonderful, women-only sex shop in New York City, calls pleasure anxiety. "When you're unaccustomed to the stronger pleasurable feelings the vibrator generates, feelings you might not have experienced before, your body may resist these feelings and create tension."

If you suspect pleasure anxiety might be a problem for you, Williams suggests reminding yourself—*repeatedly*, if necessary—that you have a right to experience such gratification. In addition, keep in mind that your body is going through exactly the same *natural* arousal experience it does whenever you're turned on—it's just doing it at a quicker rate. And the whole process won't seem so mechanical if you tell yourself that there's a person controlling the machine (you!).

Or, maybe you're scared that your new toy will work a little *too* well, and you'll become so hooked on vibrator orgasms, you won't be able to climax any other way. But those fears are almost always unfounded. "Some people do get so accustomed to vibrator stimulation that for a time they enjoy it more than any other stimulation," explains vibrator expert Blank. "But those who have had orgasms in other ways usually continue to do so with no difficulty."

Even if the only orgasms a woman has ever experienced are vibrator-induced, chances are they will only make her more eager to expand her climactic horizons with other methods. As Blank points out, "Generally, using a vibrator gives a woman confidence that her body *is* responsive, and she can go on to discover new ways of turning herself on."

And if that doesn't reassure you, your knowledge of your own need for love and intimacy with another human being—two essential things no machine could ever provide—should convince you that vibrator addiction is a truly remote possibility. Even vibrator devotee Betty Dodson was saved from going steady with her machine, she says, by a careful consideration of her vibrator's shortcomings: all buzz and no conversation—and it never initiated lovemaking!

The road to electric orgasm is paved with an enormous variety of vibrators. Some look like penises, are specifically for sexual use, and are generally sold at sex shops or through sex catalogues. Others, usually labeled "personal massagers," can be used all over the body, don't particularly look like sex toys, and are sold at most drugstores and department stores. Both kinds are also available through mail order catalogues (see page 188), so you can't use embarrassment as an excuse not to buy one!

By the way, many vibrators (especially those shaped like wands, which have a large, soft head) are *fabulous* for massage, including the everyday "my neck/back/feet are killing me" muscle aches that make you feel too tense and tired to enjoy your dinner, let alone making love. So, if you invest in a wand-type vibrator (and that's the kind I recommend most highly), don't forget to use it on *all* your body parts, especially if you need to relax before you segue into sex with a partner—or by yourself!

Employing a vibrator for nonsexual massage is also a great way to get used to your new toy before it ever comes near your clitoris. And by helping to relax you, it should make orgasm even easier to achieve. See page 190 for a rundown of the best brands, features, and approximate prices. (Like all electric appliances, always keep your vibrator away from water.)

Pump Up The Volume

Unlike Sara, Mandy had masturbated her entire life. But she had always been disappointed with her orgasms, which were only "little blips" of pleasure, far from the earth-shaking spasms other women seemed to enjoy. When she didn't have even those with her husband, it didn't seem worth the effort to try. And so faking orgasm became a way of sexual life.

But Mandy doesn't have to settle for "little blips." In fact, with a bit of practice, she can easily increase her sensations—and satisfaction, first during masturbation and later with her husband.

Most women who complain they experience only mild orgasms even during masturbation may simply be bringing themselves to climax too quickly. This can be true even if it takes you thirty minutes or more to get to that point—it's the last few minutes that are most crucial. For many women, the moments *right before* orgasm are by far the most pleasurable, but rush by in a blur before they have a chance to really enjoy them.

Luckily, there's an easy way you can learn to intensify those glorious sensations by practicing the following simple—and fun—sexercise.

Sexercise Two: Prolonging The Peak

The object of this sexercise is to learn to hold back your orgasm for as long as possible, to tease yourself unmercifully until the sensations are simply unstoppable and you *must* climax. The only two requirements are privacy and time. It is absolutely essential that you are not interrupted or hurried.

1. Begin by reading some erotic material (see Sexercise One, page 36 for some suggestions) or fantasizing freely. But don't touch yourself the moment you become aroused. Instead, let the heat in your body build until you're absolutely *aching* for some physical stimulation—even if it takes quite a while.
2. Then masturbate in whatever manner is most likely to bring you to orgasm (but don't use a vibrator if it tends to take you to the edge—and over—quickly). As soon as you feel yourself approaching orgasm, back off! Slow down, tease yourself with a lighter touch, stimulate another area that's not quite as sensitive, or even stop for a moment. Let your arousal subside somewhat, then begin masturbating again until you once more start to climb the peak. Then slow down once more.
3. If you've managed to avoid orgasm until now, you will probably be feeling frustrated *and* incredibly aroused. Repeat raising and reducing your arousal levels once or twice more until the need to climax becomes overwhelming. When you finally give in, your orgasm should be more intense than those you usually experience.

Each time you begin masturbating again, you should find yourself starting at a slightly higher

THE NICE GIRL'S GUIDE TO SENSATIONAL SEX 49

arousal level. But if you've paused too long, and your arousal has dropped back to a low point, simply start the exercise from the beginning.

In addition, it's easy to misjudge and pull back too late to prevent orgasm. If this happens, try the exercise again, trying to concentrate on the sensations you feel just *prior* to climax. It won't be long before you can pinpoint and prolong them—just practice, practice, practice until you do.

Making It Work With A Partner

Many women experience their most intense and satisfying climaxes during masturbation because of several factors: complete privacy, complete control, and a complete knowledge of what makes them feel good. Unfortunately, however, the pleasure often stops short with their own hand. "Some women separate masturbation and partner sex so completely that they would never consider trying out, in the presence of their partner, what works for them while alone," Lonnie Barbach, Ph.D., explains in her helpful book *For Each Other: Sharing Sexual Intimacy*. "Basically, they have a tendency to throw all their sexual knowledge and expertise out the window, and then wonder why they are not orgasmic with their partner."

But you can make the orgasmic leap from masturbation to partner sex with just a little thought and practice. The sexercises above helped Mandy intensify the orgasms she had during masturbation, but she was unsure how to apply what she had learned to intercourse with her husband. She knew that getting him to slow down at certain points was key and felt fairly certain she could accomplish that. But something else was confusing her. She was able to reach climax only when her clitoris was rubbed—something she knew didn't happen when her husband was inside her. So how would she ever be able to replace her fake orgasms with real ones?

There are two answers. First, Mandy—and any other woman who needs more clitoral stimulation during intercourse—can try one of what I call "the prime positions" (see page 179) that provide easy access to that little nub of pleasure so that either she or her partner can rub it (even without his knowledge in some positions, if she desires).

It's also possible to increase your sensitivity to erotic sensations *inside* the vagina, so that you can enjoy intercourse more and climax more easily.

Sexercise Three: Increasing Inner Sensitivity

According to the Kinsey Report, only 20 percent of women insert something in their vagina while masturbating, and most don't do it very often. All of the focus falls on the clitoris and therefore, once intercourse starts and most clitoral stimulation stops (unless one of you uses a hand to rub it), many women experience a deep dip in arousal. A thrusting penis just doesn't hit the spot and orgasm may suddenly seem a distant hope.

While your clitoris may always remain your sexual pleasure center, here are three exercises that will help you experience more pleasure *inside* as well.

PART ONE: KEGEL LIKE CRAZY

Back in the 1950s, Dr. A. H. Kegel made an amazing discovery. The pelvic muscle exercises he had developed for his female patients who suffered from urinary incontinence increased their erotic sensations during intercourse as well, and an incredible sexual aid was born. The exercises dubbed Kegels, strengthen the PC (pubococcygeal) muscle that forms what doctors call the orgasmic platform, and which contracts (along with other pelvic muscles) during climax. The stronger your PC, the stronger your orgasm—and perhaps your partner's as well. Some women's PCs are so developed that they can rhythmically squeeze a man's penis to orgasm *without* either of them moving another muscle!

As if that weren't enough motivation to get you to Kegel like mad, Janalee Beck, the author of *How to Have Multiple Orgasms*, insists that a toned PC is one of the essential ingredients for developing that blessed ability. So, what are you waiting for ...?

1. To find your PC muscle, begin to urinate, then stop the flow. The muscle that shuts off the stream is your PC. Start and stop a few more times to be sure you've found it.
2. When your bladder is empty, lie down, insert an finger in your vagina, and try to contract the PC muscle around it (try not to move your tummy, thighs, or buttocks). If you can hardly feel it, you have some toning to do. And even if it grabs your finger tightly, learning how to use your PC effectively will bring you much pleasure.
3. Once you've located your PC, tighten it as though you were trying to stop urination. You may feel a short surge of pleasure. Hold for a count of three, then release. Relax for three seconds, then contract again. Start with

twenty contractions, three times a day, increasing to 100 reps each time. Then, add the following variation. Contract and release twenty times *fast*, three times a day. Again, increase gradually to 100 reps.

Some sex shops and catalogues carry a metal device called a Kegel exerciser, which is shaped like a little barbell. By inserting one end (start with the slightly larger one) in your vagina and squeezing around it, you can tell if you're doing the exercises effectively. But it's certainly possible to perform the routine *without* any extra equipment.

Luckily, this is one workout that won't wear you out—if your thighs, stomach, or buttocks feel stressed, you're working the wrong muscles. Go back to the beginning of the instructions and make sure you're located the right muscle. Then try again.

Since no one can tell if you're "exercising," Kegels can be done *anywhere*. I first learned about them when I was pregnant (they also help strengthen the vagina for childbirth and return it to its original shape afterwards) and practiced on the subway, in restaurants, and at work. One friend Kegels regularly during business meetings with male colleagues. She says the secret little jolts of pleasure from the contractions and the fact that she's increasing her sexual power make her feel more powerful in general.

Part Two: Take The Elevator Up

Once you've learned to locate and tone your PC muscle, you can move on to strengthening the length of your *entire* vaginal canal with this exercise, which will further improve your grip on your lover's penis and your own orgasms.

1. To begin, think of your vagina as an elevator shaft with the elevator at the opening, the first floor. The object is to contract the muscles as you *slowly* push the elevator up the shaft to your uterus. The trip upwards should take about three seconds.
2. When you get to the top—the point where you can't contract anymore—release slowly, as if you were letting the elevator descend. Then begin again, and send the elevator up the shaft as many times as you can, building up to three sets of ten contractions each day.

If you're having trouble determining whether or not you're doing this exercise correctly, contracting around your finger can help (or ask your man to volunteer his penis for elevator duty—he'll love it). Like the preceding exercise (unless you're practicing on your lover), elevators can conveniently be done anytime, anywhere. So you have no excuse not to practice!

Part Three: Hit The Spot

Ever wish for a magic button you could press for sexual ecstasy? Some sexual researchers claim to have found one, called the G-spot, located an inch or two inside the vagina on the upper wall (the one that faces your stomach). Almost or completely invisible most of the time, during arousal the spot swells and becomes slightly raised, forming a little bump about the size of a quarter. If you can locate your G-spot by hand, you and your partner can try intercourse positions that aim his thrusting penis straight at it, resulting in an extremely intense orgasm.

Only trouble is, it's hard to find the darn thing (one reason why some researchers doubt its existence) since its location varies from woman to woman. But don't let that stop you. Send out a sexual search party (your lover can help, if you like).

1. Before you start, it's best to empty your bladder since stimulating your G-spot can make you feel as though you have to urinate. With an empty bladder, you can feel confident and not confuse the two sensations.
2. Then, while sitting or lying down (if one position doesn't work, try the other), let your fingers (or his) do the walking and explore the upper wall of your vagina, applying pressure in different spots. With the palm of the other hand, apply constant pressure on the pubic mound outside as well.
3. You'll know you've hit pay dirt when you feel a little jolt of pleasure. It may be quite subtle at first—or it may even feel slightly irritating—but stay put. As you massage (a circular motion is good), your arousal and the spot should swell, finally hurtling you into a deep orgasm that may be accompanied by pleasurable contractions in your uterus.

Or it may feel just good, but not great. To some women, the G strands for Glorious, while others feel it's not worth all the Groping needed to find it (it was actually named for Ernst Graffenburg, the gynecologist who discovered it). Either way, it pays to find out what the G-spot can or can't do for you.

G-spot stimulation certainly worked for Mandy. When she told her husband about that hidden pleasure center, he enthusiastically volunteered to lead the search. On the third try, he found it and sex for Mandy hasn't been the same since. By concentrating on intercourse positions in which her husband's penis hits the spot and which allow her room to rub her clitoris (see page 179), she no longer needs to fake an ecstatic orgasm; she has a *real* one almost every time she makes love.

Retraining Your Responses

Mandy made the transition from masturbation to orgasmic intercourse rather easily. But sometimes it takes a bit more work to make sure your climax doesn't get lost when a partner is added to the mix, especially if the way you reach climax is difficult to reproduce during intercourse. For example, if you're used to pleasuring yourself with your legs tightly crossed, by pressing your pelvis against a piece of furniture or a pillow, or even by using a vibrator, you're going to have to make some adjustments in order to reach orgasm with a partner. Luckily, although it may take a while to retrain your body, it is possible to become wonderfully orgasmic during intercourse—even if you masturbate hanging from a door—as long as you're willing to work at it.

"The most important factor to keep in mind when changing masturbation position or technique is to first discover what it is about the current position or technique that brings about the orgasm," asserts sex therapist Lonnie Barbach. "It may be leg tension, firm clitoral pressure, a feeling of safety, or the use of fantasy—to name a few. Then change the masturbation pattern in some way while trying to preserve the aspect of the pattern that is necessary for orgasm."

Sara, who had learned how to be orgasmic for the first time by using a vibrator, was thrilled to know she was able to have a climax, but confused about how to translate her new skill to intercourse *without* her electric pal. "I want to learn to have an orgasm during intercourse, but how can I without starting all over again? Unless my partner has a motorized penis, I'm in trouble." Still, when she examined her masturbation technique the way Dr. Barbach suggests, Sara realized that firm pressure on her pubic mound and intense clitoral stimulation were the keys to her climax—both of which she could achieve during intercourse, although in different ways.

Certain intercourse positions, especially those in which she is on top, will give Sara a chance to control the amount of pressure on her pubic mound, and she can get the intense clitoral stimulation she craves by using her or her partner's hand. But since fingers are far less speedy than vibrators, she must become used to building that intensity more slowly.

One way a woman can make this sort of transition is to use a vibrator almost to orgasm, then switch to her fingers at the last moment. The first time you try this, you may be able to take yourself over the edge by manual manipulation alone, but don't be surprised if your arousal level takes a sudden dip—a perfectly natural reaction to the change. You may be able to bring yourself back up to climax with your fingers, but if not, don't feel discouraged. Give yourself an orgasm with your vibrator and try again.

Once you've accomplished this last-minute maneuver, you can make the switch a bit earlier in your masturbation session, gradually moving closer to the point where you stop using the vibrator altogether. You can also try using your fingers on your vagina and keeping your vibrator on the back of your hand at the same time. That way, you can still feel the vibrations through your hand (although they won't be as strong), while you get used to stimulating your clitoris with your fingers.

If you want to change other parts of your arousal pattern—such as pressing against hard objects or crossing your legs—to make them more intercourse-friendly, Barbach insists that small changes, made slowly, have the best chances of success. "For example, if you masturbate with your legs tightly crossed, don't immediately try to masturbate with your legs wide apart," she advises. "Begin by masturbating with your legs still crossed since the leg tension this provides is probably an important factor in your arousal pattern. When you become aroused with your legs somewhat tightly crossed, reduce the crossing a bit while still maintaining the leg tension."

Retraining your body this way really works, but it often takes *weeks* (maybe more) of consistent practice before you can pull the plug on your trusty machine or uncross your legs with complete confidence. After her relatively quick success in becoming orgasmic with a vibrator, Sara became frustrated when she was unable to retrain her body to respond to her fingers with the same rapidity. But after a few months of mixed results, she had her first orgasm by hand, and soon after repeated that amazing feat during intercourse. "I almost gave up," she says. "But being able to come with a partner was worth the wait."

As you know, breaking any habit—particularly a sexual one—takes patience and perseverance. "Rather than trying something for five minutes, deciding it's hopeless when it doesn't immediately produce results, trying something else, and then giving up on that as well, pick one innovation in your masturbation pattern and stick with it," suggests Barbach. "Spend thirty to sixty minutes over two or three masturbation sessions before discarding a new technique."

If you're still having trouble with this method—or you'd like more information—pick up a copy of Barbach's wonderful book, *For Each Other: Sharing Sexual Intimacy*, as well as *Becoming Orgasmic: A Sexual and Personal Growth Program for Women* by Julia R. Heiman, Ph.D., and Joseph LoPiccolo, Ph.D.

Obviously, increasing your orgasmic ability will go a long way towards making partner (or solo) sex the ecstatic experience it can be. But in order to make the most of your new self-knowledge, you must possess the sexual confidence to put it to use—to ask your man for what you crave in bed (nicely, of course) and get it! And by the end of the next chapter, you'll know how.

3

SIX EASY STEPS TO SEXUAL CONFIDENCE

It could be the most memorable evening of your life—or the one you'd most like to forget. The sweetest man you've met in what seems like a millennium has taken you to a fabulously romantic restaurant for dinner. You've been laughing at his jokes and he's been laughing at yours, when suddenly the mood turns serious—and sexy. As the dessert plates are cleared, he puts his hand over yours and looks deep into your eyes. "Let's get the check," he whispers. "We have better things to do."

His tone makes it clear what those "better things" are, but instead of feeling turned on, you're suddenly stone-sober and *scared*. Just a few moments ago, you were marveling at how it felt like you'd known him for years. But now that it's clear this man wants to have sex with you, there's no escaping the fact that he's a *stranger*—a stranger who will soon see you without your clothes, a stranger whom you don't know how to please, a stranger who may be infected with a sexually transmitted disease, a stranger who may love you and leave you, use you and never call again. And even as you try to respond to his kisses on the cab ride back to his place, you find your confidence—and your desire—fading fast.

For many women, going to bed with new lovers is as nerve-racking as losing their virginity. "First-time sexual encounters are so anxiety provoking because they are accompanied by a long list of questions that you can't answer by yourself," explain Jennifer Knopf, Michael Seiler, and Susan Meltsner in their book *Inhibited Sexual Desire*. They claim the following puzzlers plague women (and men) most:

- Does this person find me sexually attractive?
- Will he think I'm fast and easy if I say yes or that there's something wrong with me if I say no?
- Will he lose interest in me if I don't have sex or abandon me once I do?
- What will he expect of me sexually? Will he want me to do things I don't feel comfortable doing?
- What if he's had lots of attractive, terrific lovers and I don't measure up?
- How will our relationship change if sex is added?
- How will I deal with contraception?
- Is it physically safe to have sex with him?

Any one of these questions could make you so nervous that you simply switch off your sexual desire in order to "solve" the problem. In fact, many women find themselves uncertain of their attractiveness and their partner's expectations *every sin-*

gle time they have sex—even with long-time lovers or husbands. After all, men aren't the only ones who suffer horribly from performance anxiety. They worry about their performance and we worry about our performance *and* theirs! According to Lonnie Barbach, Ph.D., author of *For Each Other: Sharing Sexual Intimacy*, "There is no other area in which everyone expects to be an Olympic gold medal winner—and without hours of daily practice, no less."

With all this worrying going on, it's no wonder that many of our sexual encounters are less than satisfying (that is, when we make it into bed at all). But it's lack of complete confidence, not lack of skill, that's often to blame.

Having sexual confidence means being able to take necessary sexual risks—whether it's trying a new partner or a new technique—to improve your sex life. (Of course, engaging in *unsafe* sex of any kind is a totally *unnecessary* risk that may end up being far more dangerous than pleasurable. See page 82 for crucial safe sex information.) It also means having the courage to communicate to a lover what makes your body sing with pleasure and what hits a sour note.

Being erotically adventurous is a state of mind that most women have to work at to achieve. We're naturally prone to all sorts of pleasure-sapping insecurities—from worrying about a less-than-toned tummy to a lack of oral sex expertise or confusion over exactly how to put a condom on a lover.

Yes, sex can be scary. After all, no other act leaves you so literally naked and vulnerable. But by taking each of the following six steps, most women can learn to overcome the fears that are holding them back in the bedroom and experience the satisfaction that only sexual self-assurance brings.

Step One: Shoot Down Your Old Sexual Image

Kelly, a 24-year-old secretary at a law firm, couldn't believe her luck. Ken, the firm's star associate, had asked her out for a fifth date (despite the fact that company policy forbade such "fraternization"). Not only was he smart and soon-to-be rich, but sexy as well, with a long, lean body that seemed better suited to a professional athlete than an attorney. From the way he touched her playfully at every opportunity, Kelly knew the evening would end in bed and that Ken would prove to be a powerful lover. She should have been looking forward to a night of pleasure—but instead, she was wondering about her own sexual prowess.

"What if he doesn't like my body? What if I can't satisfy him? I don't have that much experience and I could tell that my last lover thought I took way too long to climax," Kelly says anxiously. "And I don't really know what I'm doing when it comes to oral sex. I never know how hard to lick or suck, what feels good for a man and what doesn't. I'm Irish Catholic and my mother always said that nice girls don't need to know anything about sex to catch a man. But mom was wrong. I really like Ken and I want him to come back for more."

Jayne feels the same doubts that Kelly does, but for different reasons. She and her husband, Chip, have just reunited after he broke off a two-month affair with another woman. Despite feeling deeply betrayed and angered, Jayne's love for Chip never really wavered and now they are both committed to making their marriage work.

But the fact that Chip needed to experiment with another woman struck a severe blow to Jayne's sexual confidence, opening the door to doubts about her attractiveness. "I wonder what they did to excite each other," Jayne confides. "I've never been sexually aggressive and now I'm always worried that I'm boring Chip in bed, that it's only a matter of time until he tires of me once more." Jayne fears that if she doesn't remake herself into a sexual superstar, she'll lose Chip to another woman—this time permanently.

Many women share similar fears, as well as countless others that rip their sexual confidence to shreds. Learning how to drive men wild with oral pleasure or turning into sexual tigresses will solve only their immediate problems; these are *short-term* solutions at best.

If Kelly and Jayne continue to *expect* the worst, it's likely that's exactly what they'll get. A change in attitude—to one based more firmly on reality—is the only effective answer.

The truth is that Chip is so thrilled Jayne agreed to take him back that he'll happily return to their sexual status quo. And Ken was attracted to Kelly for over a year before he had the courage to ask her out. While he wants to make love to her, he's still haunted by the time he was in bed with a woman and lost his erection at the crucial moment.

Instead of wondering whether Kelly will be good in bed, Ken is praying his penis cooperates. As Dr. Matti Gershenfeld and Judith Newman, the authors of *How to Find Love, Sex, and Intimacy After 50* (a helpful book for women of *all* ages), point out, "No matter how frightened you are, he is probably just as frightened. After all, even though you may be worried that he won't like your body, *he's* the one who actually has to make his work."

TALK BACK TO SELF-TALK

The real key to replacing a bad sexual self-image with a good one is learning to defend yourself against the inner voice that therapists call "negative self-talk." You need to learn to curb that constant litany of self-criticism ("I'm no good in bed" ... "I'll never have an orgasm" ... "I hate my body") and replace the ego-damaging statements with self-affirming ones ("I am good in bed" ... "I can learn to have an orgasm" ... "I can improve my body and feel better about it"). Each and every time you have a negative thought about yourself, call out "Stop!" (either in your mind or out loud) and replace it with a positive one.

When this exercise was suggested to Kelly and Jayne, their first reaction was skepticism. "Sounds pretty silly to me," said Kelly, who, with only three days to go before the big date was becoming desperate enough to try anything to calm her nerves. "Ridiculous," agreed Jayne. But both had to admit it worked—after a while.

Yes, at first they felt dopey shouting a silent "stop" to their overactive imaginations like some kind of crazed thought police. But after a few days of practice, they began to control their self-talk rather than the other way around—and they began to feel more *confident*, not only in bed, but in the rest of their lives as well.

"I was so nervous when Ken undressed me that night that I started shaking," Kelly recalls. "But I just kept on telling myself that he wouldn't be making love to me if he didn't find me attractive. That enabled me to actually *believe* him when he whispered how beautiful he thought I was. And oral sex didn't even come up—so I have some extra time to practice," she laughs. "Once you master the talk-back technique it can really work wonders."

"Not being able to imagine oneself as a sexual, sensual woman makes it very difficult to be one," writes Lonnie Barbach in *For Each Other: Sharing Sexual Intimacy*. "Taking the time to create a new self-image that reflects how we would like to see ourselves ... is an important first step."

Step Two: Forgive Your Flaws— Or Hide Them

Dissatisfaction with our bodies is almost a fact of female life and a major confidence-zapper both in and out of bed. Unfortunately, almost all women are unhappy with their breasts, stomachs, thighs, derrieres, even ankles, and never more so than during sex.

This probably comes as no surprise, but what most *men* think about our bodies is a shocker! For example, many women (even those *below* normal weight) are convinced they're fat and therefore less sexually attractive. But a recent survey proved that only 8 percent of men thought their mates were too plump. In fact, some men find overweight women the sexiest of all.

In addition, women are convinced that men are breast-obsessed and believe that bigger is always better. But according to *The Kinsey Institute New Report on Sex*, "Research on what men find desirable about women's bodies has shown that only 50 percent mentioned breasts at all, and that half of those said that *small* breasts were the most desirable."

But tell those statistics to Josie and her glum response will be: "What does the research say about saggy breasts? Do men find *those* just as appealing as high, firm ones?" Ever since she gave birth six months ago, Josie has been extremely self-conscious about her flabby post-pregnancy figure and her slightly droopy bosom, so self-conscious that she's been avoiding sex with her husband Jim.

In fact, Jim does wish Josie would lose a little weight, although her plumpness certainly hasn't dampened his desire for her. And he finds her breasts, which pregnancy left softer and a full cup size larger, even more appealing than before. Yet whenever he tries to tell Josie how attractive he finds her, she refuses to trust him, adding to the frustration of both of them.

The moral of this story? Men are much more forgiving of our physical flaws than we are. So if a man says your body is beautiful, believe him! He wouldn't be in bed with you—or desperately trying to get there—if it weren't true.

Does this mean you should stop dieting or dyeing your hair? Not at all—especially if being thin and blonde improves your self-image. For *your* opinion—not your partner's—is actually the most important. In fact, you should do whatever it takes to feel better about your body short of anything potentially harmful or prohibitively expensive.

Many women want to improve their images, but actually wonder if they're worth the effort. Deep down, they may be worried that other people will criticize them for spending time and money on something "frivolous" like their looks. Dani, thirty-three and single, had always been unhappy with her mousy brown hair. She longed to be a redhead, but was reluctant to color her locks because it seemed overly vain to make such a drastic change.

Then she went to work in the marketing department of a large cosmetics company and soon discovered that many of her co-workers were not the natural brunettes and blondes they seemed to be. "One of my new friends simply said, 'Coloring your hair is no big deal. It's okay to be a little vain—in fact, it's good for you!' Then she recommended a terrific hair colorist who helped me pick out the perfect shade of red. Now I love the way I look, and I can tell men sense it. I have more dates than ever before."

As Dani discovered, a little vanity may be all you need to firm up a droopy body image. Of course, it doesn't hurt to firm up a droopy body as well. Exercise will certainly tone the flab that strikes fear in your heart each time you have to undress in front of a man. But recent research has shown that it can add more than confidence to your sex life.

According to sex therapist Linda De Villers, Ph.D., who conducted a study of eight thousand women, those who engaged in some kind of aerobic activity three times a week for three months reaped extra *erotic* benefits. Forty percent reported they were more easily aroused, 31 percent said they have sex more often, more than 25 percent claimed climaxes came faster, and 5 percent said their orgasms were more intense.

De Villers isn't sure exactly what causes this reaction, but it is known that people who exercise are less likely to become depressed and definitely have more stamina to sustain them during extended sex sessions. It's also possible that mood-boosting beta-endorphins released while working out (resulting in the so-called "exercise high") may elevate sexual desire as well.

But one thing is certain: When you see the results of exercise, you begin to feel better about your body and yourself. And so it's natural to feel more desirable!

That confidence increases the longer you stick with an exercise program. Fitness experts report that women who work out regularly have an easier time accepting their bodies' flaws because they feel they have some control over them. They've been able to firm their flabby stomachs and reduce large thighs so they know they can deal with minor defects.

That was certainly the case for Josie. She had been considering having plastic surgery on her breasts when another new mom urged her to join a special postnatal aerobics and muscle toning class at the local YWCA. Inspired by the instructor who had borne three children and managed to maintain a flat stomach, and swept along by her compatriots in the class, Josie committed herself to three sessions a week. Her instructor explained that since breasts are mostly fat, not muscle, it's not possible to tone them. But it *is* possible to tone the pectoral muscles *underneath* the breasts by lifting light weights, which would help make them look less droopy.

Josie had her doubts, but decided to suspend them for a one month trial—and by then, she was hooked. Her thighs no longer rubbed together, her tummy began to tighten, and her breasts appeared firmer than before. And it was no coincidence that as she regained her body confidence, her sexual desire returned as well. She and Jim still have to deal with the enormous stresses of first-time parenthood, but resuming their sex life has certainly helped.

Could exercise restore *your* sexual confidence? It's worth a try, and with the wide variety of available options, it's easy to find one that will work for you. Some women adore the structured atmosphere of a health club with a wide variety of exercise machines and regular aerobics classes (not to mention all those cute guys running around in spandex pants). Others would rather go it alone with a workout video at home, avoiding the crowds and the cost. Most important is choosing an activity you enjoy so much you *almost* become addicted to it. If you like walking, for example, simply speed up and push yourself for longer distances.

But don't overdo it. Incessant exercise can backfire, disrupting your reproductive cycle and possibly causing amenorrhea (a condition where you stop menstruating) that may also cause vaginal dryness and inhibited orgasm (difficulty reaching climax). You have a problem if you find yourself choosing to work out instead of going on a date or spending time with your spouse, or if you exercise even though you're injured or sick.

Creative Camouflage

If sweating your way to a sexier you sounds totally *unappealing*, you may just have to accept that you'll never love the way you look naked. So, don't fight it, *hide* it! The enormous variety of gorgeous lingerie available can disguise almost any body flaw and certainly distract from those it can't.

A red satin teddy or a corset can hide a thick waist; lace-trimmed tap pants or bloomers can conceal cellulite-ridden thighs; black stockings with a sexy back seam and a garter belt can cover those little blue spider veins that men never notice but women do; and an alluring push-up bra (with peekaboo cups, perhaps?) from Frederick's of Hollywood can certainly draw attention away from an overly ample bottom. And almost any woman can transform herself into a sex goddess by slipping into one of those merry widows that Madonna made so popular. It conveniently covers flaws and flab while emphasizing your most alluring curves.

Best of all, lingerie is sanctioned by the top sex therapists as an effective sexual confidence booster. "It's like a beautiful, carefully wrapped gift," says Dr. Barbach. "The attractiveness of the package makes the unwrapping a special pleasure in itself." Of course, you can stay at least partially wrapped even *during* lovemaking if you desire—but make sure you're sexually accessible. For example, wear your pretty lace panties *over* your garter belt, so they can be removed easily or your poor partner may become crazed trying to find a way to penetrate you.

With all the teddies, camisoles, corsets, tap pants, petticoats, silky slips, and negligees (seethrough and otherwise), how's a girl to choose? Cynthia Heimel, the author of the hilarious and helpful *Sex Tips for Girls*, suggests: "When buying lingerie, think filthy thoughts, and think about men. And don't think you're some kind of nonfeminist reactionary sniveling turncoat for doing this, because you're not. Turning a man on as much as possible is beneficial to both concerned." So leave your politically correct considerations by

THE NICE GIRL'S GUIDE TO SENSATIONAL SEX 71

the front door of Victoria's Secret, and grab a shopping cart!

If you have any doubts about what kind of lingerie your lover prefers, try taking him shopping (after you both have a stiff drink). He might be a little flustered at first, but he'll warm up as long as you remain by his side (men have a tendency to panic when they realize they're embarrassingly alone in the bra section).

Encourage him to pick out his favorites and limit try-ons to one session at the end (try to sneak him into the booth to test your choices' arousal quotient. But don't be surprised if he pleads for a "quickie" right there. As you'll see, a skimpy piece of satin or silk can be a powerful aphrodisiac!).

Another plus of taking your lover shopping is that he'll probably pay (men love buying lingerie), but if not, never purchase anything so expensive that it can't be *torn* off your body. That, after all, is part of its purpose!

Dress For Sexcess

Your lover may never be motivated to uncover your tap pants and teddy if they're hidden by the pair of sweats and old t-shirt you normally wear around the house. It's possible to be comfortable—and sexy—at the same time. And it *does* make a difference. He certainly won't love you any less if you dress like a slob, but he might forget there's an alluring body under that ratty, stained bathrobe.

If you usually wear:	Try:
Baggy sweats	Curve-hugging leggings
Cotton panties	Lace bikinis (with a cotton crotch)
Granny-style night gown	Satin nightie or *nothing*
Pantyhose	Stockings and garters (at least once in a while)
No makeup	At least a touch of lipstick
No earrings	Small diamond studs (fakes are fine) or at least a dab of perfume on each lobe
Gooey night cream	A light moisturizer that *disappears* into your skin
Old, holey, ratty *anything*	Clean, new *everything* that he'll see you in (more than worth the investment)

When buying clothes, why not think sex—at least some of the time? Even if you have to dress conservatively at work, wear cuts and materials—cashmere, silk, lace, velvet (or their cheaper, but still soft, synthetic equivalents)—that make it clear you're not just one of the boys. No, I'm not encouraging you to look like a slut, just to reflect your own personal definition of sexy.

If you're the sporty type, choose the same

sporty-style dress you feel most comfortable in, but try a more *clingy* fabric. If you lean towards the classic look, try leaving an extra button undone on your blouse or wear a slightly shorter skirt and higher heels. Even little adjustments can add a lot of *ummph!*

Allowing yourself to feel sexy and enjoying men's appreciative looks isn't sinful *or* antifeminist (after all, if Gloria Steinem wears body-hugging blouses and mini skirts, why can't you?). And it doesn't mean you're asking to be sexually harassed (if that were true, the sexiest thing a woman should wear is a potato sack). It just means you feel good about your body and yourself—an essential element of sexual confidence.

Whether you opt for lacy undies, a sexy silk blouse, or a slimming exercise routine, don't feel guilty for wanting to look your best. Some people may say that you shouldn't need to rely on such "devices." But if you use them to jump-start your self-confidence, after a while, you'll find you no longer depend on them—that you can be a sex goddess without a perfect body, and radiate erotic allure in even the sloppiest pair of sweats. You'll finally believe you're a sexy woman—and you'll be one.

Step Three: Help *Him* Get A Grip

You may be confident of your status as a sexy person, but is your partner confident of his? Probably not. He may seem the definitive stud, but underneath, his penis is like putty in the awesome grip of a performance anxiety that's far worse than yours. According to Bernie Zilbergeld, author of *The New Male Sexuality*, "Control and predictability are crucial to us, yet in sex we are dependent on an organ that often seems to have a mind of its own, totally beyond our attempts to direct it. This does not feel right or good. We fear that, sooner or later, it is going to disappoint us."

If you can put your lover at ease, you will have his undying gratitude—and a much better time in bed. But the best perk of all is that by bolstering his confidence, you'll also bolster *yours*. And it's easier than you'd think.

"Will it stay up?" is usually a man's primary concern, with "Will I be able to satisfy her?" running a close second, and "Will she reject me if I don't?" bringing up the rear. In addition, a friend who's a successful veteran of the dating wars points out, "Sex is the ultimate intimate experience, and women are a lot more comfortable with intimacy than men are." Recalling one man who insisted on making love in the dark, and another who felt comfortable after sex only if he put his underwear back on the moment he withdrew, she says, "Merging so completely with another human being makes some men *very* nervous."

In fact, men are even more vulnerable than we are in this area, and it doesn't take much to make a man's sexual confidence—and therefore his penis—poop out. "Male insecurity is caused by anything that makes a man feel unimportant, undesirable, not quite adequate," explains Zilbergeld. "Sex is just like sports—people don't perform well when their self-esteem is low."

But don't expect your lover to 'fess up to feeling less than confident. Because most men have bought into the myth that they should always be ready, able, and willing to have sex, few feel comfortable admitting that just isn't so. Men aren't supposed to be unsure of their lovemaking skills or insecure about their bodies. Yet they do have many of the same fears as women—they just suffer in silence.

There's no hiding a penis that fails to rise to the occasion, although some men have certainly tried (you should be suspicious if your lover suddenly flips over on his stomach and refuses to budge). But there are other, less obvious signs that your beau is having a confidence crisis. He may perform mechanically, unable to relax and let go. He may be reluctant to try a new technique for fear of failure. He may even start faking orgasm—thrusting like crazy as though in the throes of climax and then pulling out before he *falls* out! (Unfortunately for men, they're at a major disadvantage in the faking game. If you have any doubts about whether he actually ejaculated, simply insert a finger in your vagina and take a whiff. Semen has a recognizable, slightly ammonia-like odor.) Or the poor dear may start avoiding sex and even hugging and kissing because he's afraid affection might lead to a command performance he's not sure he can deliver.

But you can rescue him before things go that far. As Kelly found out the first night she spent with Ken, you don't have to know how to use your tongue like a call girl to help your lover keep his erection and confidence up (although it never hurts!). Your enthusiasm is far more important than your sexual skill. *Nothing arouses a man as much as a woman who is obviously aroused by him.*

I'm not telling you to fake your responses, but don't hide them either. When you first glimpse his pride and joy, there's nothing wrong with giving a little gasp of surprise and saying something like: "You're so much bigger than I expected!" If his touch pleases you, let him know with a little moan.

If not, move his hand away gently, but try to avoid snapping, "Will you please stop that!", especially if this is one of your first times together.

Begging and pleading for more also go a long way with a lover, especially if you let him know you don't beg and plead for just any man. Men love cheerleaders—and not just because they wear such short skirts. That "You can do it" attitude is highly appealing. (No, you don't actually have to shout out, "Go, Jack, go!" in time with your lover's thrusts—a sweet little moan here and there to let him know he's doing a great job will suffice.)

"The first time we made love, Ken kept telling me how beautiful I was and it made me feel wonderful," Kelly says. "So I decided to do the same for him. Our next date was right after he had lost a major case and I knew he was feeling low. So when we made love, I made sure he knew what a winner he was in bed. I'm too shy to say much out loud, but I tried to swallow my inhibitions and urge him on. Being so good for each other's confidence has really brought us closer."

Taking any or all of the actions above will do as much for your confidence as his. But perhaps nothing will increase your sexual assurance as much as allowing yourself to be truly active in bed. Contrary to our fears, men aren't threatened by aggressive women, they're usually turned on by them—at least in bed. Society has conditioned men to believe they must always make the first move. But when you take the lead and show your lover how turned on he makes you feel, it relieves that awful pressure, allowing him to relax and blissfully surrender control.

In the end, there's nothing like watching a man go wild from the touch of your tongue or hands to convince you of your own formidable sexual power—so don't let this fabulous confidence booster go to waste.

Step Four: Nurture Your Sexual Ego

Once you've planted the right seeds for sexual confidence, you must tend it like a fragile flower—at least until it's strong enough to stand up to the inevitable storms and dry spells on its own. The following dos and don'ts will give it the best chance of survival.

1. DO go to bed with a new man for the right—or at least clear—reasons. Take some time to find out if your new lover is healthy, heterosexual, single, and wants the same things you do from the encounter. If you suspect he's simply looking for another conquest while you're looking for a lasting relationship, stop and ask yourself why you're spending the night with him.

Of course, there's nothing wrong with having sex for purely recreational reasons. Letting your lust run wild in a steamy affair not only feels stupendous, it can increase your feelings of desirability and prevent you from becoming just a little too desperate to fall in love.

As long as you're clear about your motivations—and make it a point to *always* practice safe sex—you'll be able to enjoy the experience without any awful morning-after regrets.

2. DON'T let the first time be the last. The first time you have sex with a man you really do like—could possibly even love—can be particularly harrowing. The heroes and heroines in romance novels may melt together in instant, sizzling ecstasy, but in real life, the lovemaking is more likely to be anxious and awkward until you get to know each other's sexual ins and outs.

As a result, this delicate situation deserves a do and don't list all its own:

Don't rush it. If mutual lust lands you in bed on the very first date, fine. But don't let a man lead you there against your wishes (only a jerk would try to do that). According to a sex survey by *Cosmopolitan* of its readers, only 1 percent of women have sex on the first date, while a whopping 71 percent wait until the third or fourth, with the rest putting it off even longer.

Of course, fear of AIDS is a major reason for the delay, but it's not the only one. As the survey pointed out, 72 percent of *Cosmo*'s readers said that waiting helped them know their partner better—and 52 percent claimed the anticipation also made sex even more exciting.

This same caveat applies to the big night itself. Don't let his arousal hurry you. Instead, prolong it for both of you with some delicious preliminaries. Slow dance to sexy music while you sing something sultry in his ear. Neck on the couch for a while. Then undress each other *slowly*.

Do plan ahead. One unbreakable rule: Eat lightly if amour is on the agenda. As you may already know from experience, too many burritos and boisterous sex are an unfortunate combination. In addition, try to limit yourself to no more than a margarita or two (no matter how nervous you are). Too much alcohol may calm your nerves, but it will also dull your arousal and responses. And it would be nice to remember what he was like in bed so you don't have to go through the "first time" all over again on your next date.

It will probably also make you feel more comfortable if your introductory encounter takes place on your own turf. So make sure to suggest your place before he suggests his, and do a little pre-date prep. Put clean sheets on the bed, make certain there's something edible in the fridge (sex makes some men ravenous) and that your birth control is handy (the time to search for that misplaced diaphragm is *now*), hide your copy of *Women Who Love Men Who Hate Women*, and make sure your tub is free of scum and stray hairs (you never know when you might want to take a steamy shower *à deux*).

Do admit you're nervous. There's nothing wrong with confessing you're a little scared or shy. In fact, your partner will probably find this sort of admission rather sweet and endearing and do his best to set you at ease. It will also stop him from wondering if all that shaking is simply nerves or a symptom of some dread tropical disease.

Do be responsive—but don't show off. Perhaps after reading this chapter, being nervous is no longer a problem. In that case, be just a bit cautious—or you might scare *him*. If you have a few sexual tricks up your sleeve, go ahead and give him *one* as a treat. But, as Cynthia Heimel points out, "Erections have a way of shrinking when confronted with circus acts." So save the rest (especially anything involving whips, handcuffs, or dildos) until you're a bit better acquainted.

Don't expect grand passion at first. Few women climax the first (or even the second, third, or fourth) time they make love with a new man, so don't put unnecessary pressure on yourself. And while it's okay to act a bit more excited than you actually are, it's best not to start off a fresh sexual relationship by faking an orgasm. Chances are, he'll be way too bashful to ask if the earth moved or not. If he does, I love this advice from an article Susan Shapiro wrote for *Cosmopolitan:* "Tell him you make a point of never coming the first time. If you can't help yourself, then feign shock and tell him it's the first time you've ever come the first time."

3. DON'T fall for unfair criticism. When Nina, a book editor, first met Bob, a movie producer, she was immediately attracted to his powerful good looks and the way everything about him said "success." Riding in his black Porsche and entering an outrageously expensive restaurant on his arm wasn't only fun, it made up for all those dateless Saturday nights in high school, and it made Nina feel good about herself.

But soon after they began dating, Bob began criticizing. At first, it was little things that he made loom large, like the time she was five minutes late or the too-bright color of her lipstick. Desperate to please—and hang onto him, Nina vowed to be on time and wear paler lipstick. But it wasn't long before Bob was telling her she was stuck in a dead-end job or too dumb to understand a political conversation he was having with his friends—or that her lack of sexual expertise was causing *his* impotence.

"I wanted to marry the guy, so I told myself he wasn't really being cruel," Nina recalls. "And I almost quit a job I love just to please him. But one night he couldn't get an erection and he blamed me as usual. Well, I tried rubbing and sucking and everything I could think of for more than an hour and nothing worked. And when he finally pushed me away, all he said was 'You call yourself a real woman? You can't even make a man hard!'

"Suddenly, something in me just snapped and I was able to see him as the pathetic, whining failure he really was. I got up out of bed and I never went back. Thank God," she manages to smile. "Or I might still be spending my nights trying to gauge my self-worth by the stiffness of his penis."

As Nina discovered, if a man is a constant criticizer—in or out of bed—stay away, even if he's a sexual superstar. Don't allow him to feed his own shaky ego by taking big bites out of *your* self-esteem.

4. DON'T let rejection ruin your sex life. It's happened to all of us—but that doesn't make it any less heart- or ego-breaking. The marvelous man you slept with twice has suddenly stopped calling. The sex was great, the conversations were even better ... so what happened? And how can you stop the pain?

First of all, take a hard look at the situation. If you can't think clearly, ask a girlfriend who likes you enough *not* to lie to help you. If the relationship was short and mostly sexual, you may have missed some signals your lover was sending that he intended to keep it that way. If you're honest with yourself, you'll probably find you were ignoring the fact that there was actually no deep connection between you or that he had a history of behaving this way with women but you didn't want to believe he would behave this way with *you*.

But even if the reasons he rejected you remain a mystery, don't let fear of a repeat performance keep your bed empty. Most sexual rejections have nothing to do with you. Your hit-and-run lover may be terrified of commitment, still nursing a broken heart from a past relationship gone wrong, or simply interested in adding another lover to an already long list of conquests.

Just because you didn't win this particular male booby prize doesn't mean you're a sexual loser. It does mean that perhaps you should move a little more slowly next time and invest a little less of yourself emotionally *until* you know what type of man he is.

Don't be afraid to put off having sex with a new man. If he tires of the delay and disappears, you have your answer.

Step Five: Protect Yourself Against Pregnancy And STDs

By its very definition, confident sex is *safe* sex. It's impossible to concentrate on pleasure and perform at your peak if you're scared of pregnancy or disease. But, for some reason, many smart women make foolish choices when it comes to birth control and STD protection. Deborah, 27, had been using a diaphragm ever since the gynecologist at her college student health center had decided that it was the best birth control choice for her. In fact, Deborah didn't like this method at all, and so consistently made mistakes that could result in pregnancy. She did insert her diaphragm each time she had intercourse, but she never applied quite enough spermicidal jelly—especially around the all-important rim—to create a sperm-proof seal. And she ignored instructions to insert extra jelly the second time she had sex the same night.

THE NICE GIRL'S GUIDE TO SENSATIONAL SEX 83

"Using all that jelly makes it really messy," Deborah explains. "Even after I remove the diaphragm the next morning, the jelly continues to drip, drip, drip out of me all the next day. I hate it."

Billie, 30, had also been dissatisfied with her contraceptive, and after finally breaking up with a cheating boyfriend, had no intention of sleeping with anyone else, at least for a while. "I'd been using the pill for seven years and thought this might be a good time to give my body a break from it," she explains. "I decided to think about other birth control options."

The trouble was, Billie never quite got around to choosing one, and after two months of celibacy, found herself in bed with a new man and *no* birth control. "We met at a party and were instantly attracted. We left together and rented a ritzy hotel room for the night. I assumed he would have condoms, but he didn't. It was 2 a.m. and all the drugstores were closed. We were crazy with desire, and I didn't want the opportunity—or the beautiful room—to go to waste. So I decided to take a chance and use nothing."

The decisions that Deborah and Billie made were the wrong ones, and both paid dearly—Deborah with an unwanted pregnancy and Billie with chlamydia, a sexually transmitted disease. Although both women are organized and more than competent at work and in the rest of their lives, neither took the time or the trouble to choose a birth control and STD protection method that would work for her *in every situation*.

Yes, protecting yourself from pregnancy and disease can be expensive, messy, and certainly the last thing you *want* to think about when your lover has just unhooked your bra and is busy covering your breasts with butterfly kisses. Luckily, you won't have to—if you've given your choice some careful consideration long *before* you end up in bed.

BIRTH CONTROL: HOW'S A GIRL TO CHOOSE?

While no form of birth control (even sterilization!) is completely infallible, almost all can be highly effective at preventing pregnancy. But that effectiveness is almost entirely determined by *you*. If you rely on a method that goes against your personality or is too much of a hassle, you're likely not to use it correctly—or perhaps at all.

For example, the diaphragm has a failure rate of only 6 percent *if* it's positioned correctly and you use enough jelly. If you skimp, however, like Deborah did, the failure rate zooms to 18 percent, increasing your chances of becoming pregnant to almost one in five. Deborah played birth control roulette and lost because she chose a method that was totally wrong for her.

If you're confident in your current method—and you use it consistently *and* correctly—let the lovemaking begin! But if not, it's time to look deep into your soul—and body—and ask yourself the following essential questions (be honest, now!):

1. Do you have sex more than twice a week?
2. Do you tend to have more than one steady partner?
3. Are you likely to have intercourse more than once each night?
4. Are you sometimes so "swept away" by desire that you're tempted to skip birth control "just this once"?

THE NICE GIRL'S GUIDE TO SENSATIONAL SEX 85

If you answered *yes* to all four questions above, your active sex life and low tolerance for interruptions calls for a silent partner like the Pill, an IUD, or possible Norplant implants (six small capsules that are inserted under the skin of your upper arm in a fifteen-minute procedure at your doctor's office. The capsules then continuously release levonorgestral, a hormone also used in oral contraceptives, for up to five years).

If you answered *no* to all four questions, a diaphragm, cervical cap, or a condom may be more your sexual style—especially if you're wary about anything that tampers with your reproductive system, no matter how safely. And if your answers and your situation change frequently, you're going to have to choose even more carefully.

Many women I know use the Pill when they're actively dating, then switch to a diaphragm when they enter a long-term relationship and feel comfortable enough to interrupt foreplay briefly to insert it. (By the way, a diaphragm doesn't *have* to be messy. Just make sure you don't overdo the jelly or cream—check the manufacturer's recommendations—and, after you withdraw the diaphragm, simply use a sanitary napkin or panty liner to catch any leaks or drips.)

Now ask yourself one last question: Does your current method best match your sexual personality? If not, it's time for a change. Ask your gynecologist what options she or he recommends. But it's up to *you* to make sure your new method is the right choice for your lifestyle.

Whatever contraceptive you pick, make a commitment to use it *religiously*—then forget about it, confident in the knowledge that it will be doing its job while you enjoy yourself!

THE CONDOM CONUNDRUM

No matter what kind of birth control you use and how faithfully you use it, only a *latex* condom lubricated with the spermicide nonoxynol-9 will help protect you and your partner from catching one of the more than 30 STDs (sexually transmitted diseases) out there, including the AIDS virus. (Lambskin or "natural" condoms prevent pregnancy, but are too porous to protect against STDs.) That means that if you're having sex with anyone but a long-term and compulsively faithful partner, you must use a latex condom *in addition* to the Pill, diaphragm, or any other contraceptive.

And that condom should go on your lover soon after his penis becomes erect—before it touches your mouth or vagina. According to a new study by the Brigham and Women's Hospital in Boston, it's possible for a man's pre-ejaculate (that tiny bit of fluid that seeps out of the tip of the penis long before orgasm) to contain HIV-positive cells *if* he's infected with the AIDS virus. That means that *you* could become infected if you swallow some of that fluid during oral sex or if you put his penis in your vagina during foreplay. Since a man is unable to sense when he's about to release pre-ejaculate, the earlier the condom is in place, the safer the sex.

STD protection seems logical, but sex often defies logic. That's why many men don't spend much time thinking about condoms, and often consider birth control and STD protection a woman's responsibility. According to *The National Survey of Men*, a 1991 study of the sexual behavior of 3,321 American men between the ages of twenty and thirty-nine, only 52 percent of single men under thirty use condoms regularly, and that number drops to 36 percent for those over thirty.

While there are many guys who use condoms every time they have sex, too often they rely on the woman to carry them. "Most of the girls I know keep condoms in their pocketbooks or medicine cabinets," says Donald, a 28-year-old banker. "I figure that if a woman wants me to use one, she'll provide it. Besides, the risk of getting AIDS is really low."

You should not be taken in by such careless thinking, so be prepared to supply protection when you're with a man. The key word here is "risk," and there definitely is one. So why take a chance?

Condoms used to be cool (historic super stud Casanova reportedly considered them essential equipment for any sexual rendezvous). And before the age of AIDS, when a rubber was simply a cheap form of birth control, every teenage boy carried one in his wallet, desperately hoping for the chance to use it. But today, these same men are more likely to "forget" to bring one to bed.

According to several studies, there are three main reasons for this strange "condom amnesia":

First, many men (and women) feel rubbers are unromantic because of what they *represent:* nasty, unsexy STDs. It's the *idea* of the condom, not the latex itself, that interferes with their emotional pleasure.

The solution? An *essential* attitude makeover. "Learn to love latex," the wise Dr. Ruth Westheimer advises in *Dr. Ruth's Guide to Safer Sex.* "If you associate the look, feel, taste, and smell of condoms with great sex, they will become sexy."

That's not that hard to do, as you'll soon see.

Colored and flavored condoms can add a touch of all-important playfulness to your next tryst, while those that are ribbed can increase vaginal stimulation during intercourse (not a bad perk!). And once you learn how to roll on a rubber correctly (instructions are coming up in a moment), you can make it a regular part of your foreplay and be done with it in a flash.

Some men also worry that wearing a condom will reduce the sensations they feel during intercourse and make it harder to maintain an erection. This is true for many who have had the ego-bruising experience of losing their erections in the middle of making love. As a result, they're afraid to do anything that might cause them to "lose it" once again. Men in their forties and fifties may also fear that a condom will reduce the friction they need to stay hard during intercourse, and resist your efforts to make them wear one.

So what can you do when your lover starts to put up a fight the moment you suggest slipping him into one of those little ribbed numbers you've come to like so much? Pull out two! According to Dr. Ruth, many men report that wearing a double layer of condoms (lambskin underneath, latex on top) creates even more of the friction they crave.

In addition, you can let your reluctant condom wearer in on a little secret: While condoms do reduce sensation a bit during intercourse, they may also prolong the pleasure by delaying ejaculation, as half the men who responded to a *Consumer Reports* readers poll discovered.

If your lover is still opposed, let him know that *you* won't be able to be as relaxed and responsive without the security of a condom, and he'll have far less fun as a result.

THE NICE GIRL'S GUIDE TO SENSATIONAL SEX   89

Finally, many men are embarrassed about buying condoms (it's true!). As I'm sure you've learned by now, if a man finds anything even slightly embarrassing, he's highly unlikely to do it. That means that you'll have to be the one to supply the condoms, either by going to the drugstore or a sex shop, or ordering them through the mail. Yes, always having to be the partner in charge of birth and STD control is a pain. But at least you'll know that you'll have a condom when you need one, and that you're completely confident of your own protection.

Sex would certainly be sweeter if you didn't have to worry about STDs. But you *do*. "Because condoms help prevent STDs, they also help prevent conditions in women that result from STD infection, such as pelvic inflammatory disease (PID), which in turn can lead to ectopic pregnancy and infertility," advise the scientists from the Battelle Human Affairs Research Centers who conducted *The National Survey on Men*. "Condom use may also protect women against cervical cancer."

Ironically, once you accept that condoms are here to stay, safe sex is actually the most *liberating* kind. For slipping on that simple sheath of latex is the only way to truly free your mind from fears of deadly disease not only *during* sex, but on the morning after as well when you don't have your lover's delicious kisses to distract you.

So do yourself and your partner a favor and always make love according to the following credo: No condom, no sex.

A PROPHYLACTIC PRIMER

Luckily, prophylactics have come a long way since the days when Dr. Condom first provided them to England's virile Charles II in an effort to stem the steady flow of his illegitimate offspring. High technology has made condoms thinner, stronger, sexier, and sometimes sillier. A bestseller at Condomania, a chain of stores in Los Angeles, New York and Miami which stocks a whopping 209 varieties, is the Knight Light, a neon green number that actually glows in the dark. Condoms also come in red, yellow, blue, even black, and an astounding cornucopia of gourmet *flavors* that sound more like they belong on an ice cream cone than a penis. Orange, banana, strawberry, chocolate, mint, passion fruit—take your pick. (Call 1-800-9CONDOM for a free copy of Condomania's mail order catalogue.)

Unfortunately, while these flavored condoms can give oral sex a tasty twist, most *don't* protect against pregnancy or STDs, and lack FDA approval. If a condom box is marked with the words "sold as a novelty," that's *all* they should be used for.

Never fear, however. Manufacturers offer a head-spinning assortment of effective latex condoms spiked with spermicide—ribbed or smooth, snug fit or *extra* large (a sure man-flatterer), nonlubricated or extra lubricated for women (complete with a pink carrying case). You can further customize with a water-based "condom flavoring" product. Two companies, ForPlay and Kama Sutra, offer such choices as mandarin orange, wild strawberry, cappuccino, and vanilla cream. (Kinda makes you wonder what will be next!)

If your needs are a bit more basic, two of the best—and thinnest—regular condoms are the Skin Less Skin, made by Okamoto, a Japanese company, and the Gold Circle Coin, made by Safetex in the

USA, which has been rated Number One by *Consumer Reports* and packaged to resemble those chocolate coins you found so yummy as a kid. Sold in drugstores across the country at around 50 cents apiece, the Gold Circle Coin is a birth control bargain.

If you're a bit nervous about someone (maybe Mom?) spotting a condom wrapper when you open your purse, many companies are now producing stylish "condom carriers." Some look like small makeup cases, others like pretty jewelry or key chains featuring a hidden condom compartment. Since jewelry is usually the last thing a woman slips off before she slips into bed, these carriers are especially convenient (which means you're more likely to use what's in them).

There are, of course, a few places *not* to keep your condoms. Heat and light weaken latex, so don't store them in your car's glove compartment or anywhere else they'll be exposed to high temperatures (get your lover to find a place other than the wallet in his back pocket for the one he likes to carry—long-term exposure to body heat is also bad). If stored properly, condoms should last five years. Always check the expiration date before you buy—and don't purchase a package without such a date.

How To Put The Darn Thing On

Your "no condom, no sex" rule will be a lot easier to enforce if you're able to entice your partner with a sexy (and effective) "placement procedure." In addition, your doing the honors will take the pressure off him and make him feel positively worshipped.

First of all, make sure your condom supply is close by where you can find it fast (your lover may lose patience as well as his erection if you need to spend several minutes searching your sock drawer), and that you have more than one on hand.

But don't whip out your Rough Rider (a studded condom made by Ansell Incorporated) right away. If he's not completely hard, he's not ready for it anyway. Instead, the idea is to *integrate* the act of putting on the condom with the rest of your lovemaking—and make it just as sexy. So stiffen him up a bit with some teasing touches before your reach for a rubber. (Not only will this make it easier to get the thing on, but he'll be so delirious with desire he won't waste time objecting.)

When he's ready, unwrap the condom carefully (no biting the package!) and place it on the tip of his penis. (If he's not circumcised, pull the foreskin back.) Then start unrolling it down the shaft *slowly* to make sure it isn't inside out. (If it is, it'll start rolling back on itself. In that case, it's best to toss the condom and start over with a new one.)

If you're using a plain-tip condom (a look at the package will tell you), don't pull it snug against the head of his penis. Leave about a half-inch free at the tip to collect the semen, and pinch the end to get rid of any air bubbles. If the condom has a reservoir tip, give it a firm squeeze to eliminate air bubbles, and you're ready for action. Just press your fingers lightly against the rubber's bottom rim as your lover penetrates you to make certain it doesn't roll back up. Then let go and forget about it!

If you're using spermicide, put a dab inside the tip of the condom before you put it on your lover, then slather some more on the outside before he enters you. Most spermicides also do double duty as a lubricant.

After he's ejaculated, have your lover withdraw *while he's still hard* in order to prevent leaking. Once again, hold your fingers around the rim as he does, and then be polite and help him off with it. The condom will probably be a sticky, unsightly mess, but don't rush the removal process or you're likely to catch some of his pubic hairs as you roll down (ouch!). When it's off, simply tie a knot in the top and toss it *(not* down the toilet, where it's sure to clog things up).

If you're a bit unsure of yourself, buy a box of condoms and practice on a banana (the salesman at Condomania says most cucumbers are probably too large in circumference). When you're ready to test your new skill on a penis, try to keep your sense of humor—and your cool—and watch those nails! It won't be long before you're a pro.

Step Six: Learn How To Ask For What You Want—And Get It

The first six or seven times Mary Ann, 26, and Joe, 27, made love, she was still high from the influence of that most mind-altering of all legal substances: a blossoming romance. All her thoughts about sex were directed towards pleasing her brand new boyfriend, and she didn't think much about her own sexual satisfaction. "I was still basking in the fact that this incredibly attractive man seemed to be falling in love with me even faster than I was falling in love with him," Mary Ann explains. "I wasn't having orgasms in bed, but I didn't really mind. I figured the sex would just get better as we got used to each other."

As time went on, Mary Ann and Joe did grow closer and closer emotionally, but not sexually. Although Joe desperately wanted to be the best lover Mary Ann had ever experienced, his efforts were mostly hit or miss. "He'd start off rubbing my clitoris nice and slow," Mary Ann reveals. "But then, just as I'd feel this delicious orgasm begin to build, he'd speed up like a madman, then stop altogether and enter me. Changing the rhythm and then abandoning my clitoris like that just left me hanging there—really aroused but unable to climax, and feeling extremely frustrated. But I was too worried about insulting him to tell him what was wrong." Instead, Mary Ann would sneak out of bed after Joe was asleep and masturbate in the bathroom.

Laura, 26, also longed for a different kind of loving from her boyfriend Todd. While she almost always had an orgasm when they had sex, she craved the type of intense climactic ecstasy she had experienced only once before—when a previous lover had performed cunnilingus (oral sex) on her. That other man had dived head-first between her thighs without even asking, and, to her surprise, had seemed to actually enjoy kissing her "down there." Laura had enjoyed it too. And the amazing things he had done to her with his agile tongue had left her gasping from pleasure and made an impression that haunted her whenever she made love with Todd. "I've never felt that way again," she recalled wistfully. "And since Todd doesn't seem to be interested in doing that sort of thing, I guess I never will."

It was true that Todd's mouth had never yet ventured lower than Laura's breasts, but, then again, she had never asked him to. Fear choked her—fear that her vagina smelled and tasted bad, fear that her desires were somehow abnormal, and fear that Todd would brand her a slut for having them.

"Perhaps my last lover was a real sexual weirdo," she reasoned, "and he managed to turn me into one too." So Laura remained silent—and frustrated, forced to miss out on incredible sexual pleasure because of an all-too-common lack of communication.

Unfortunately, the sad situation Laura and Mary Ann are in is far from rare. Many women have found themselves in a similar sexual bind, and a large percentage of them have remained unsatisfied in bed not just for a few months at the beginning of a relationship—but for years and years of marriage. Even if you've been mum about your own needs and desires for *decades*, however, it is possible to finally learn how to ask for what you want in bed—and get it.

A recent survey by Philip and Lorna Sarrel, two Yale University sex therapists, concluded that "the ability to share thoughts and feelings about sex with your partner is the single factor most highly correlated with a good sexual relationship." In fact, this study has only proved the theory that every therapist on the planet has been pushing for years: that open communication is the key to stellar sex—*and* a rock-solid relationship.

Luckily, your man is on your side. Like Joe, most men are extremely eager to please when it comes to sex. He may never learn how to load the dishwasher correctly no matter how much you nag, but gently hint that using a bit more suction on your nipples will send you into spasms of lust, and his mouth will be on your breasts before you can finish your sentence.

The reason: there are few things more ego-gratifying or arousing for a man than knowing that he's the stud responsible for setting you on fire. (Think how fabulous *you* feel when your touch makes him groan with desire!) The more orgasms a man "gives" his partner, the greater the boost to his sexual self-esteem. So, it's obvious that making sure your lover possesses the knowledge necessary to achieve this feat will be of great benefit to *both* of you!

Without your guidance, the poor fellow is likely to try whatever made his last lover moan (and she might have been faking!) or just do whatever feels good to *him*. That was Joe's strategy. Too afraid to ask Mary Ann if he was turning her on—in case the answer was no—he simply treated her clitoris the same way he liked his penis handled, and hoped for the best.

But the best is not to be—at least not until Mary Ann learns how to communicate her desires to Joe. Rather than remain silent and unsatisfied, Mary Ann and any other woman who wishes her lover would do more of this and much less of that can increase her pleasure in bed by following the four rules of great sexual communication below. As you'll see, you can even learn to ask for what you want without ever saying a word out loud if it makes you too uncomfortable (this technique is a bit tricky, but it *can* be done!).

RULE #1: CREATE YOUR OWN SEXUAL WISH LIST

The first person you need to ask about what you really want in bed is *yourself*. Like many women, you may feel you "need more stimulation" from your partner, but exactly what do you mean? Do you want your lover to go faster or slower, harder or softer, touch lightly until just before orgasm and then apply more pressure—or just the opposite?

If you've never thought specifically about what you need, now's the time. Therapists suggest creating your own sexual wish list on paper to clarify your needs. Think about what usually happens—or fails to—in bed, and be specific about what you'd like your lover to do differently. If you think you know what's wrong, but not how to fix it, you may need to spend some more time exploring exactly what satisfies you sexually so you can pass that knowledge along to a partner. If that's the case, reread the last chapter and try repeating some of the sexercises.

Rule #2: Politeness Counts

If, like Laura, you know exactly what you'd like your lover to do more—or less—of, but have been too shy or embarrassed to ask, let me assure you that there are many ways you can make a sexual request without being whiny, ego-bruising, or slutty. As in most things, it's the *way* you ask—not what you ask for—that counts.

Whatever your request, make sure the words you use are polite and positive, without a hint of criticism. For example, if you want your lover to go more slowly, rather than saying, "Don't rush me," rephrase your request in a more positive manner by stating, "I love it when you take your time..."

Similarly, rather than using a phrase like "I find the way you're rubbing me a bit irritating," *redirect* his efforts to a body part that would appreciate the attention by whispering, "If you want to drive me absolutely bonkers, try *gently* rubbing me here" or "I just love it when you..." and move his hand to the new spot. That way, instead of feeling badly about doing the wrong thing, he'll simply be happy—and relieved—to discover something else that really makes you hot.

One woman I know wanted her clitoris rubbed in a very specific way, but was too embarrassed to demonstrate the technique herself or guide her lover's hand "down there." Instead, she said, "Let me show you how I love to be touched," and demonstrated the soft, slow, circular motions she craved on her lover's arm. Her boyfriend didn't need to be shown twice. He was thrilled to be told how to give her pleasure in such a nonthreatening way, and her little lesson had *lasting* orgasmic consequences.

Laura, on the other hand, was not able to be brave enough to voice her request until her boyfriend opened the door to better bedroom communication. As their love deepened, so did their trust in each other, but their lovemaking remained routine—until Todd had the courage to voice his own request. One night as they were smooching passionately under the covers, Todd whispered something Laura didn't catch. When she asked him to repeat it, he asked in a small, halting voice, "Would you kiss me down there?"

Pleased to try something that would turn him on, Laura nodded yes—and saw her opportunity. "I will if you will," she replied.

"I think that can be arranged," Todd replied, grinning. "I've been dying to go down on you, but since you never asked, I was afraid you didn't like it."

Laura quickly reassured him, and a few minutes later, she was experiencing the exquisite pangs of pleasure she had craved for so long, while giving as good as she got, as she and Todd lay in the 69 position. That night, both the sexual *and* emotional bonds between them were strengthened.

Men often seem to feel a bit more comfortable making sexual requests, so if your lover asks for a special favor, seize the opportunity and pipe up with your heart's (or body's) desire.

Another good way to open up the lines of sexual communication is to ask your lover if there's anything wonderful you can do for him. This will lead him to ask if there's anything wonderful he could do for *you*, and *voila*, you've created the perfect opening to voice your own desires.

RULE #3: IF YOU CAN'T TELL HIM, AT LEAST SHOW HIM

Learning how to make a sexual request is an important skill every woman should master. But if that seems a truly impossible task (at least for now), there are several nonverbal ways of communicating your wishes. One simple way is to leave your wish list on his pillow (make sure it's worded extremely kindly and that you aren't bombarding him with *dozens* of requests). Or you can try leaving a sex manual where he will find it, open to a page with a position or technique you want to try (for more on this approach, sometimes called bookmarking, see page 126).

Many women (and therapists) also swear by what one friend of mine calls "the great sex switcheroo." Instead of telling your lover what you want, let him know you're going *show* him by making love to his body the way you want him to make love to yours. Obviously, this role-reversal technique does have its limitations, but it's extremely effective for getting across the message that you like your strokes slow and soft, for example, rather than hard and fast the way he does. When he's had his lesson, encourage him to take a turn on you and you'll learn something too!

Mary Ann tried this technique on Joe, who finally learned she likes slow strokes all the way to orgasm. When they switched roles, she discovered that he liked his nipples sucked, something he'd been a bit embarrassed to reveal. This new knowledge was very empowering for both of them. "We're still not completely in sexual sync," Mary Ann reveals. "But we're much closer to getting there. I'm starting to have orgasms with Joe, and now I know how to drive him even wilder with pleasure."

RULE #4: LET HIM KNOW IT'S WORKING

When your partner *does* strike the right tempo or discover the perfect stroke, don't forget to reward the industrious lad with an enthusiastic response! "More, more!" or "Yes, yes!" will certainly let him know he's on the right track, as will periodic passionate moans of pleasure.

And don't forget the compliments if you'd like a repeat performance. Be lavish with your praise and you can be sure he'll store his newfound, precious knowledge for future use.

This whole chapter was designed to help you travel the sometimes rocky road to sexual confidence. Now you're ready to explore a fabulous new frontier: fantasy land. As you'll soon see, it's definitely worth the trip!

4

FANTASY FUN: NAUGHTY *AND* NORMAL

"It's sunset and the beach is beautiful, the sea and sand bathed in a rosy gold glow. I'm lying alone, on a large, soft towel, with my eyes closed, waiting for my boyfriend Philip. I'm nude and my skin feels wonderfully warm from the sun. No one else is around for miles.

"Then I sense a man's presence behind me, and a second later, I feel Philip's hands on my hair, massaging my head. His hands move down to my breasts, which tingle from his touch, and then his lips are on mine, drawing me into the most luscious, sensuous kiss I've ever experienced. It's slow, teasing, incredibly arousing—and not Philip's style at all. That's because, as I suddenly realize, it's not Philip who's kissing me. I'm unable to open my eyes to confirm it, but I know that some man I've never met is about to make love to me—and I'm more turned on than I was before.

"I reach for him, desperate to touch his body, but he grabs my wrists and whispers harshly, 'Don't move.' I should be upset by the fact that he's forcing himself on me, but I'm not. I feel wonderfully free and sexy and light as he continues to expertly caress me—somehow still holding my wrists immobile.

"By the time he finally lowers his body on mine and enters me, I'm panting with desire. I come almost immediately, and then it feels like his hands, mouth, and penis are all down there at once. The sensations are fantastic and I have one orgasm after another after another.

"At that point," Jill continues, "I usually have one or more orgasms in real life too. And when I finally open my eyes, I feel a little bit surprised that I'm at home masturbating or having sex with Philip. I also feel pretty guilty for having cheated on my boyfriend that way. He'd be terribly hurt if he knew what I did to make myself come. Plus, I'm letting myself be raped in my fantasy. What's wrong with me?"

The answer is: Absolutely nothing.

Until 1973 when Nancy Friday published the first ever collection of female sexual fantasies in her book *My Secret Garden*, most men *and* women didn't think we had such lusty imaginations. But endless studies since have shown that the female fantasy is alive and well in America, and that most women regularly indulge in erotic reveries—during masturbation, sex with their partners, and many times throughout each day in nonsexual situations.

Everyone has sexual fantasies, even though many of us might not think they're sexual. But just wondering how good it would feel to make love to or even kiss someone is a sexual fantasy.

And contrary to a popular—and rather harmful—belief, imagining you're being pleasured by

THE NICE GIRL'S GUIDE TO SENSATIONAL SEX

another man—or even a *group* of men—while you're masturbating or having sex with your mate doesn't mean there's anything wrong with your real-life sexual relationship or with *you*. In fact, such steamy daydreams are almost crucial to a healthy sex life.

That's not surprising since your brain is your most important sex organ, refusing to let your other body parts become turned on unless it is too. When anything gets in the way of that arousal, upwards of 80 percent of all women call fantasy to the rescue. And an effective white knight it is, shielding a damsel in distress from all sorts of obstacles that try to stand between her and orgasm.

Each woman's private sexy scenarios are as personal as her fingerprints. But most do fall into general groups by subject, forming a sort of female fantasy hit parade. Here are the current top ten (the exact order of popularity isn't known):

Favorite Female Fantasies

- Being forced to have sex
- Making love with a movie star, former lover, friend, co-worker, relative, or stranger
- Having super sex with your present partner
- Being the star of a threesome or group grope
- Dominating a man and controlling his climax
- Playing a stripper or prostitute
- Having sex in an exotic and/or public place
- Being satisfied by an expert *female* lover
- Having intercourse with a horse, dog, a gorilla, or other animals
- Being spanked or otherwise physically punished for being a "naughty girl"

What Turns *You* On—And Why?

Why does one woman reach new erotic heights at the thought of being chained and "tortured" to climax while another dreams of doing the dominating—literally whipping her lover into an orgasmic frenzy? Why does one become aroused at the idea of being a high-class call girl who "services" hundreds of men, while another regularly reaches orgasm while imagining her superbly skilled lover is another woman—even though she's strictly straight? Why does one dream about making love to a movie star, while another does it with her dog (more popular than you'd think!) in her fantasies? No one really knows, but that hasn't stopped experts—and everyone else—from trying to guess.

Some psychologists believe that adult fantasies are closely linked to early sexual experiences. "Many fantasies have their basis in incidents occurring in early childhood or adolescence when sexual feelings were high and a real understanding of sexuality was very limited," asserts Dr. Lonnie Barbach in her book *For Each Other*. "An early spanking that was coupled with sexual feelings might persist in fantasy many years later. Peeking in a half-opened door and watching a couple make love might reappear in later life as voyeuristic fantasies. Feeling turned on by fantasies of being forced to have sex could stem from our adolescent years when, in order to maintain our reputation, we had to fight our boyfriends at each step of the highly sexually charged exploration."

But other experts argue that a woman's steamy reveries have more to do with her *current* sexual and emotional needs. Most female (and male) fantasies are probably a combination of both, a search for solutions to sexual issues past and present—with a little kinky fun thrown in. Jill's fantasy of being "raped" by a stranger is a perfect example.

Bye-Bye Guilt, Hello Orgasm

Like so many of us, Jill was brought up with the words "Nice girls don't let boys touch them" ringing in her ears. Before she left on dates as a young teen, her mother always reminded Jill that it was her responsibility to control the sexual urges of the boy she was with and protect her virginity. Her mother never told Jill how to control her *own* urges, however, and her silence on the subject made Jill think she was the only one who tingled when a boy did manage to get his hands on her breasts, and that those tingles were *bad*.

That early chain of guilt maintained a stranglehold on Jill's sexuality. And though she eventually dated and slept with many men, her mother's words always came back to haunt her subconscious and held her back from enjoying herself fully in bed—until Jill broke free by developing her fantasy. By imagining that she's helpless to stop the stranger's seduction (he holds her wrists and some magic power has made it impossible for her to even open her eyes), she can't be held "responsible" for the incredible ecstasy he "forces" on her. As a result, Jill is able to maintain her "nice girl" status—and enjoy a series of stupendous orgasms.

Unfortunately, a new guilt—over what her fantasy means—has replaced the old. Like Jill, the millions of women who have this most popular of all female fantasies sometimes worry that just because they're turned on by the idea of being "raped," it means it's something they'd actually want to experience in real life. And for those who consider themselves true feminists, the fact that they're excited by the idea of a man overpowering them can be extremely disturbing.

Rikki, 32, is a police detective who prides herself on being just as macho as the men she works with. She's had to put up with a lot of teasing since she joined the force of a large East Coast city ten years ago. Her male counterparts simply didn't believe "a pretty little thing" like her could hold her own on the city's tough streets, and they let Rikki know it.

"I've had to prove myself over and over," Rikki says. "I had to show that I could take control of any situation, that I wasn't afraid to tackle even the biggest male perp. Now that I've made detective, I feel I've finally achieved the respect I worked so hard for, which is why I'm so appalled with where my mind goes during sex.

"I have this fantasy where I'm abducted by this drug dealer I've been after for over two years in real life. I'm about to arrest him, when he somehow turns the tables on me and ties me to this bed with my legs spread wide open. He makes me drink something and it's this drug that turns me into a nymphomaniac. It makes me want sex desperately, even with this ugly man I hate. I just can't help myself.

"I'm crying as he tears off my uniform, begging him not to do what I know he's about to, but he doesn't listen. All he says is, 'You know you want it, bitch. You've wanted it for a *long* time.' He puts his head down between my legs and starts to use his tongue on me and the pleasure is excruciating. I try to struggle, but it just feels better and better, until I come like I never have before," Rikki pauses, looking a bit ashamed of herself. "I guess, deep down, I'm terrified that's what I really want."

But therapists insist such fears are almost completely unfounded. "Many people don't realize that what is arousing in fantasy may in no way indicate what would turn them on in real life," explains Barbach. "A woman who finds a rape fantasy erotic is very unlikely to have the same response were she to be actually raped." In fact, Rikki's fantasy may just be her mind's way of relieving some of the enormous pressure she's always under by allowing her to lose control *safely*, without real life repercussions.

In addition, the idea of being taken by force can sometimes boost a woman's self-esteem as well as her arousal. Nina, whose former boyfriend Bob had criticized her about everything from her eating habits to the shape of her breasts, found herself plagued by doubts about her sexual attractiveness and fears that she would never find another partner. "Then one day, while I was masturbating, this image of this devastatingly handsome man—the type of man who could have any woman—popped into my head," Nina recalls. "We're at a party and he's asked me to dance. The music has a heavy, sexy beat and he draws me into his arms.

"It isn't long before I feel his erection pressing against me and then he's whispering in my ear that I'm the sexiest woman he's ever seen. I try to pull away, but he's holding me too tightly. Part of me is mortified, hoping the other people dancing won't notice. But another part is electrified with desire. He's rubbing his pelvis against me in time to the music. And then he says that he must have me, that he's never wanted a woman so much, that

I'm impossible to resist. Again, I try to struggle, but he's too strong, and no one seems to be aware of what we're doing. Then suddenly he's inside me, thrusting hard, and I'm so aroused I feel like I'm going to faint.

"I don't know what happens after that, since I've usually come by this point," Nina says. "But that fantasy leaves me feeling like a sex goddess who can conquer any stud out there."

Fear Of Fantasy

Some women are so afraid they might act out fantasies they consider morally wrong that they try to block them from their minds (only to have them intrude more often, of course!). Others worry that fantasizing about another man while having sex with your partner is equivalent to actually cheating on him. "I use that beach fantasy so often, it almost seems like I'm having an affair," Jill confesses.

If this is a fear of yours, give yourself some credit. Fantasies simply have the power to arouse you, not to make you *act*.

When should you worry? There might be some reason for concern if the *only* way you are able to respond to your lover is by fantasizing about someone else—especially if it's a man you know.

Dwelling on erotic thoughts about your brother-in-law, your boss, or anyone *but* your current partner can cause guilt, which can definitely interfere—or even stamp out—sexual pleasure. No, you shouldn't feel guilty—the difference between imagining and doing is *everything*—but try sticking to strangers.

If the everyday mystery man doesn't do it for

you, try a movie star. Whenever a sexy male star opens in a new movie, he can be found in the beds of thousands of women later that night. Research in the 1970s revealed that Robert Redford, Paul Newman, and Tom Selleck were the most popular fantasy figures. Today, it's probably Tom Cruise, Kevin Costner, and Mel Gibson, although we won't know for sure until yet another comprehensive research study confirms it!

Other women dream up scenarios in which they are seduced by someone they swear they'd never be attracted to in real life: an ugly co-worker, their husband's pudgy best friend, even their priest or rabbi! There's no need to worry—your mind is just playing with some interesting "What if . . ." situations. Always remember that *you* are the director of your own mental movies. So if you find the male lead or any other element of your fantasy disturbing, you can simply yell: Cut!

The only time fantasies can truly cause trouble is when the film keeps rolling and rolling despite your efforts to stop it. "In rare cases, a person can become so fixed on a particular fantasy that he or she cannot become aroused without it," explains Dr. Miriam Stoppard in her book *The Magic of Sex*. "While a fantasy that exercises such a strong hold can be very useful during masturbation, it can get in the way of shared sexual activities. Instead of concentrating on how your partner is reacting, and what you can do to please him or her, you can become fixed on bringing your fantasy to life, and thus seem remote and nonresponsive."

The majority of women, however, are more likely to indulge in fantasy too little, rather than too much. Always remember that it's *100 percent normal* to be sexually attracted to other people.

That attraction does *not* mean you no longer love your man, that you're a slut in the making, or that you're likely to act on your private thoughts.

Most of the time your common sense and conscience will be more than enough to keep you in line. So don't feel guilty no matter what erotic images you conjure up. By barring sexual boredom from your bedroom door, fantasies may actually help you and your lover remain faithful to each other.

What Another Woman Knows

Many heterosexual women are puzzled—and sometimes deeply disturbed—when their fantasies include being pleasured by a *female* lover, but this situation is more common than you'd think. Annie, the graduate student you met in Chapter Two, often finds herself daydreaming about being expertly brought to orgasm by another woman, even though she's never had a same-gender experience and feels very certain she wouldn't want to.

"In my fantasy, I've had an awful day at school and I'm taking a hot bath to relax," Annie relates. "I settle into the water, but I can't seem to get comfortable. All my muscles ache and my head hurts where it's lying against the tub. I'm squirming around, feeling very sorry for myself, when I hear a warm voice say, 'Here, let me help you.'

"I look up and Miss Bracken, my high school drama teacher whom I really adored, is standing by the side of the tub. She looks just as I remember her—young and pretty, with dark, dancing eyes and this beautiful auburn hair—and she's dressed in a terry robe.

"Before I can answer her, she rolls up a thick,

soft towel and puts it under my neck. Then she takes this beautiful green bottle out of her pocket and tells me to close my eyes, which I do. A moment later I feel her reach down into the water and start to spread this silky green lotion all over my body from my head to my toes. It's soothing but also extremely sexy.

"When her fingers start massaging between my legs, I tense up a little bit—not because she's a woman, but because it usually takes me such a long time to climax and I don't want to displease her. But just as though she can read my mind (and I guess since this is a fantasy, she can), she tells me not to worry, that she has all the time in the world, that she loves pleasuring me like this.

"Miss Bracken's fingers feel so delicious, and somehow, while she's rubbing my clitoris, she's massaging the rest of my body as well—and every touch is in exactly the right place. Soon, with no effort on my part, I'm coming in a way I never have with my boyfriend. My whole body feels like it's having this enormous orgasm. It leaves me totally limp and completely happy."

Does this fantasy mean that Annie is a latent lesbian? Probably not. More likely it reflects the fact that Annie has been having trouble achieving climax with her new boyfriend Mark, who likes sex a lot rougher and quicker than she does, and her longing for a lover who would handle her more gently and patiently.

According to experts, women often seek out in fantasy what they aren't getting from their lovers in real life. A female lover's appearance in a straight woman's scenario may express a longing for more tenderness from her current male partner and a fervent wish that he knew instinctively how to pleasure her (the way another woman would) *without* having to be told. Since men haven't been blessed with such sexual ESP (if only they *were!*), it's no wonder so many women turn to the same sex for satisfaction—at least in their imaginations.

A Truly Useful Tool

As you can see, fantasy is one of the most effective (and certainly cheapest) sexual aids. Here are just a few of the other ways these erotic reveries can make a major difference in your sex life.

- **Fantasies fulfill a basic *biological* need.** While men tend to focus on brief, explicitly erotic images, women often draw out their daydreams into full-blown and extremely detailed scenarios—complete with steamy dialogue and romantic touches—that let the sexual tension build *slowly*. This reflects both a woman's emotional and physiological needs. Because it generally takes a woman longer to become aroused and reach orgasm than a man, an unfolding story gives her as much time as she requires.

The ability to create such a detailed daydream can come in handy. Lisa, a 35-year-old office manager, is married to Larry, a 40-year-old electrician. "He's the sweetest man in the world," Lisa says, "but the worst lover. His idea of foreplay is a few French kisses. Then he's on top of me, pumping for a mere minute or two, and it's all over before I know it. He gives me another kiss and rolls off me, and he's snoring peacefully ten minutes after we began.

"I wish I had the courage to say something," Lisa confesses. "But there are so many things wrong I wouldn't know where to start. And I love him so much that I would never want to hurt him—but I don't like going to bed feeling frustrated either. So I developed this technique. While Larry is still watching the ten o'clock news in the living room, I get into bed and start having sex all by myself. I fantasize about Larry, who really is still quite sexy-looking, but in my fantasy, he's a real *stud* as well.

"I dream we're in a sumptuous hotel room in Paris, complete with a round bed with satin sheets. He's undressing me slowly and tenderly, planting fiery kisses along my bare flesh. Then we fall together on the bed, sliding across the smooth, silky sheets, rolling over and over, just reveling in the feel of our hot bodies pressing against each other. After many long, intense kisses, he whispers, 'I'm going to make love to you all night.' And then his mouth is down between my legs and the feeling is fantastic and just goes on and on and on.

"I picked this story up from one of my favorite romance novels, but it really works for me. I touch my breasts and vagina very lightly and teasingly during the whole thing, and by the time the news is over and Larry comes to bed, I'm more than ready for him. In fact, I'm dying to have intercourse hard and fast, which is exactly what he does. I have a climax almost every time this way, and if I don't, I wait until he's asleep and then finish myself off."

Yes, it would be better for both Lisa and Larry if she let him know how she really longed to make love, and she *should* learn how to communicate her needs and desires. But in the meantime, her fantasy is helping her out of a tight sexual spot.

- **Fantasies help you stay focused during sex.** Too many women zone out during lovemaking, letting their minds drift to the deal they're trying to put together at work, where they can find shoes to match a new dress, even what to get their sister for her birthday. Unfortunately, distractions have a way of diluting sensations so that even the most exquisite touch feels simply "nice."

As I mentioned before, your brain needs to be fully engaged with sexy thoughts before it will let your body respond. Your man could be an amazing lover, but if you're thinking about what to plant in your vegetable garden this spring, everything he does will be for naught—leaving you both feeling frustrated. Fortunately, fantasy is an easy way to bring your mind back to sex *fast*—and keep it there.

"I used to be easily distracted when Rich and I made love," Terri says, "especially when I was tired and had a thousand things to do the next day. But when my lack of interest in sex began to hurt my marriage, I decided to see what I could do to keep my attention focused on the matter at hand.

"Because I take a 7 a.m. aerobics class three times a week, I'd often find myself thinking about it while I was making love with my husband the night before—wondering whether I had a clean sports bra to use and if my worn-out sneakers would last through another workout. I'd try to pull myself back, but nothing worked for long—until I incorporated the exercise class into a fantasy.

"I would imagine that Rich and I were top sexual athletes and had been asked to instruct the class in our superb technique. We had to demonstrate our mastery of all sorts of complicated and physically demanding positions. The idea of all these people watching us perform was *very* arousing—and it was a great segue back to sex.

"I haven't let Rich in on my secret—yet. I just bought a few sex books and told him I wanted to try some new positions. He loves the variety, and I get to act out my fantasy," Terri says with a sly smile. "Needless to say, I'm no longer distracted. In fact, these days I can hardly keep my mind *off* sex!"

- **Fantasies intensify arousal.** In order to get the most enjoyment out of any sexual encounter, you need to concentrate on fulfilling *your* sexual needs as well as your partner's. This is not the same as *worrying* about whether they will be fulfilled. As most women know, anxiety and arousal don't mix well. The more you worry about reaching climax, the less likely you are to actually find yourself there.

Fortunately, fantasies can distract you from your distractions. According to Dr. Stoppard, fantasy "helps to focus our attention on our own sexual responses, making them larger than life, and encourages the brain to respond even more enthusiastically to the signals of arousal it is receiving. It then sends out hormones that increase the excitement in our genital organs."

In fact, in some cases, *fantasies can make the difference between an incredible climax—or none at all.* If you always reach orgasm during masturbation, but never during intercourse, fantasy may be what's missing. Some women simply refuse to accept the fact that they need fantasy to push them over the edge—no matter how much they love their partners. Held back by the belief that fantasizing during partner sex is "perverted" or that their lover should be enough to arouse them, they stifle their fantasies *and* their sexual feelings.

This was the case with Amanda, a client of psychologist Lonnie Barbach. "Amanda could have orgasms through fantasy alone, without any additional physical stimulation," Barbach reports in *For Each Other*. "However, she had never had orgasms with her partner. When I asked her if she ever fantasized while making love with a partner, she told me that she would never allow herself to fantasize with another person present because she felt it wasn't normal. Her partner's physical presence should be enough.

"However, after finally accepting the idea that it was perfectly normal to fantasize, she decided to try it during partner sex and, to her surprise, had no difficulty attaining orgasm."

If you find yourself squelching your own steamy reveries—and possibly your climax in the process, try *consciously* fantasizing while you make love. Replay an old favorite to see if it does the trick—you have nothing to lose and an orgasm to gain!

- **Fantasies allow you to explore all sorts of sex acts *safely*.** Human beings crave novelty in most areas of life, and sex is no exception. Once unleashed, even the average imagination can come up with some extraordinary erotic daydreams. But just because you're curious about what it might be like to be chained to the office water cooler and forced to perform oral sex on your boss and the rest of the sales staff doesn't mean it's something you would enjoy in real life. That's where fantasy comes in. According to *The Kinsey Institute New Report on Sex*, it can provide a "safe way to experience situations an individual would never actually do."

Susie, a 27-year-old receptionist, has a fantasy that both excites and scares her. It all began when she and her husband, Ryan, a 28-year-old computer programmer, decided to take a Caribbean cruise. "At meals, Ryan and I were seated at the same table as another couple our age, Tom and Janine," Susie explains. "We got along great, and ended up spending a lot of our time on the boat together, sunning ourselves out on the deck. Janine and I were both wearing really skimpy bikinis and I'd often catch Tom staring at me and Ryan staring at her. I liked the attention, and I felt safe flirting back because I knew it couldn't go any farther—I would never have an affair.

"But then, one day, it did. The four of us were lounging by the pool. I needed to get some more suntan lotion from our cabin, and Tom said he wanted to go back to his to take a shower. He followed me down the deck, and as soon as we were out of sight of our spouses, he pulled me around and kissed me. Somehow I wasn't surprised because I had felt an intense attraction between us all week. And even though I knew I was in the arms of another woman's husband, I found myself kissing him back and pressing against his body.

"It never went further than that kiss—I guess we just needed to let off some sexual steam. But after that, I started fantasizing about having wild sex with Tom while Ryan made it with Janine. Throughout the whole trip, I had sensed they were attracted to each other as well, and, strangely enough, it didn't bother me the way I would have sworn it would.

"Instead, all the erotic electricity really turned

me on. At first, in my fantasies, I never saw Ryan and Janine, although I 'knew' they were doing all sorts of naughty things to each other in the next room. But recently, I've been imagining that all four of us are in the same bed having an orgy. I find the *idea* of group sex extremely arousing, but I don't know if I'd actually want to try it in real life," Susie confides. "I'm afraid it would hurt my marriage, or that it would be humiliating and I'd hate myself afterwards." As long as it stays in her head, however, Susie need never fear. For one of the great things about fantasy is that you can experience the excitement *without* worrying about the consequences.

Fantasizing is also an excellent way to explore a sex act you feel certain you *would* like to try. Kelly, who was dating Ken, wanted to perform oral sex on him, but was worried she wouldn't do it correctly. One evening while she was daydreaming about their next date, her thoughts drifted to exactly what she wanted to do to him.

In her mind, she was an expert at "going down" and drove Ken crazy with ecstasy. "I went through it step-by-step, imagining how I would slowly unzip his pants, tease him with my tongue until he couldn't stand anymore, then take the head of his penis in my mouth, and bring him to orgasm. When he came, I even pictured myself swallowing his semen without a problem. My fantasy was sort of like a mental dress rehearsal," Kelly says, "and it gave me the courage to try it the next time we were in bed together. Ken was quite pleased!"

- **Finally, fantasies can make you better in bed.** Being a good lover means being an active sex partner, participating fully in a joyful search for pleasure, rather than lying back passively and simply *hoping* it happens. Fantasies are a way you can take responsibility for arousing yourself and making sex better for you.

Your lover will never know your secret thoughts unless you share them (more on that later), but he'll certainly share the benefits. There is nothing sexier than a lusty woman who is obviously interested in pursuing pleasure (it's no coincidence that such a female is often the main figure in *male* fantasies!). The more aroused you are, the more he will be too, and the less pressure he'll feel to perform—making him a better lover as well.

Finding Your Way To Fantasy Land

Some women are master sexual storytellers, spinning long, steamy tales to add spice to their sex lives. Others concentrate solely on the pleasure of their physical sensations while making love and feel no need for fantasy. But many could use a boost in bed and have never even tried this marvelous sexual device—or have reserved it for masturbation alone. (If you get more satisfaction from sex with yourself than with a partner, the fact that you don't fantasize during intercourse could be a big part of the problem.)

Luckily, it's easy—and a lot of fun—to develop your erotic imagination. The best way to begin is by imagining that your lover is willing to pleasure you any way you want—and that he's tireless. Set aside some private time to plot the perfect lovemaking scenario, drawing out every sensual detail of the who, what, and where. Are you at the office, in a romantic restaurant, on the beach? How do his lips taste when they first touch yours? How does he smell? How do his hands feel on your body—and more important, what's he doing with those hands?

You can also base your imaginary adventure in real life, by thinking back to an occasion when the sex you had was the hottest ever. If you can remember all the details, make them even more exciting with a little erotic embroidery. If not, just make them up! After all, that's what fantasy's all about.

In addition, there's nothing wrong with "borrowing" someone else's fantasy or using it as a jumping-off point for your own. Renting an X-rated video can provide you with a treasure trove of exciting ideas. Some directors, such as Candida Royale, are trying to make erotic movies with plots that appeal more to women. You can also read over the erotic reveries of the women interviewed for this chapter or pick up a copy of one of Nancy Friday's voluminous female fantasy collections: *My Secret Garden*, *Forbidden Flowers*, or *Women on Top*. (Not a bad idea if you're still worried about the "weird" content of some of your own mental images. You'll quickly see that many women have far kinkier minds than yours.) They should give you a lot to think about!

Here are some other hints to help you better integrate your imagination and your sex life:

- If you've never fantasized before, try it first while masturbating. It's easier to coordinate your movements with what's going on in your mind than it can be during partner sex.
- The first time you try to fantasize during partner sex, start your scenario *before* your partner ever touches you (the way Lisa does

with her quick-loving husband Larry), so you'll be well into it by the time you begin to actually make love. Then try consciously adding bits of your favorite fantasy here and there. For example, when your partner enters you, conjure up the way it happens in your daydreams, "combining" the two for an extra erotic charge. Don't worry if you feel awkward at first or you have trouble getting the action in your mind and your bed into sync. Keep trying and soon it will be second nature.

- Don't stick stubbornly to the chronology in your fantasy story. Be ready to hit rewind or fast-forward to keep pace with your partner.
- Enhance your arousal even more by using your mind's eye to take a peek at what your body is doing. Studies have shown that women who climax most easily have discovered a fail-safe technique. They pretend they're part of their own X-rated video, which they're starring in *and* watching at the same time. If you'd like to try the same trick, try mentally zooming in on a shot of your lover's mouth teasing your nipples, his penis thrusting, even what it looks like when he's ejaculating inside you. Such potent images are sure to intensify your physical sensations.

Can You Make It Real—
And Would You Even Want To?

Often the key to a fantasy's sexual power is the fact that you're dreaming of a forbidden act—something that you would never actually do. Therapists have found, for example, that women who try to make their fantasies real by actually having sex with a stranger or another woman or an animal can end up more confused than aroused. Thinking about such acts may be a turn-on, but really doing them can be a definite turn-off.

But almost every woman will enjoy acting out certain *elements* of even the kinkiest fantasies—especially in the safety of a trusted lover's arms. By diluting a full-strength fantasy down into something you *can* handle, you decrease the danger while increasing your excitement.

When Barb was having sex, for example, her mind always seemed to drift to the same fantasy, one that so shocked this mild mannered 27-year-old executive assistant that she would never dream of telling her boyfriend about it. Still, she longed to actually experience the *feelings* the fantasy aroused in her.

"My fantasy takes place in a dungeon with dozens of men chained to the walls," Barb reveals shyly. "You're not going to believe this, but I'm their jailer and I control them *completely*. I don't need a whip or any weapon to do it. Just a harsh look from me is enough to make a man whimper and behave.

"I make my rounds completely naked (in my fantasy, my body is *fabulous*, firm and lush), caressing a chest here, a thigh there, arousing the whole crowd until they all have enormous erections. But they know the rules: If a man so much as touches his penis, I have to punish him severely. So all the prisoners are trying to resist, even though the sight of me is driving them crazy.

"Finally, I come to my favorite prisoner. His heavily muscled arms strain against his shackles as I approach and a lock of his long blond hair falls over his face, but it doesn't hide the raw sexual hunger in his eyes. I'm a tiny woman, but as I brush my breasts casually across his chest, I can feel this big man shiver with lust, and I know he's totally in my power.

" 'Let me serve you, mistress,' he begs. But I silence him with a kiss. Just as he leans into it, however, trying to assert himself, I pull away, and slowly run my tongue lightly along his body, teasing one nipple and then the other, and finally gliding down between his thighs. I take his penis into my mouth, and he groans with gratitude. But I suck on it for just an instant before popping it out. My prisoner thrusts his hips forward wildly, trying to find my mouth again, but I won't give him the satisfaction.

"Instead, I take a step backwards and begin to pleasure myself in front of him, coming closer and closer to climax as he watches and becomes more and more aroused. The great part is that he has absolutely no hope of release—unless *I* allow it.

"It's only after I've had several orgasms that I take a gold key from around my neck, unlock his chains, and finally put him out of his misery. I push him down to the dirt floor and mount him. And with him thrusting like a bucking bronco beneath me, I bring us both to a final, crashing climax."

Is Barb a budding dominatrix? Not likely. But her fantasy does reflect her wish that she could assert herself more in the rest of her life. Although she makes a respectable salary as the assistant to the CEO of a Fortune 500 corporation, Barb often wonders if it's worth it. Her sadistic boss takes great pleasure in dominating her, sometimes forcing her to do menial tasks such as polishing his shoes or pulling apart the paper clips that he obsessively chains together. And if Barb so much as frowns at one of his orders, he gleefully reminds her how easy it would be to find another assistant. So Barb ends each day furious with him and herself, feeling overwhelmed and unable to control her life.

But in her fantasy, *she's* the one in power. And while Barb was correct that her boyfriend Sam wouldn't have reacted well to the idea of her being aroused by dozens of men (none of whom are him), she was surprised to find that he was willing to go along with her general desire to try domination.

In fact, being forced to surrender control is possibly the most popular male fantasy. Barb made the discovery that one of Sam's favorite erotic scenarios complemented hers almost by accident, when she was undressing in front of him one night. "I had removed all my clothes and was unwinding a scarf from my hair when Sam suddenly held out his wrists in front of me," Barb explains.

"It took a moment for me to realize what he wanted me to do. But then I took a deep breath and tied the scarf around his wrists and wove it into the bars of our brass bed. Then I used two other scarves to tie each ankle to a bedpost. When I saw him spread-eagled on the bed, completely vulnerable—and erect—it was like a dream come true. I was in complete control of the man—I decided when he could touch me, when he could touch himself, even when he could come. It was the best sex I've ever had, and, strangely enough, it helped me deal with my awful boss the next day."

THE NICE GIRL'S GUIDE TO SENSATIONAL SEX

Should You Share?

Barb found herself in the enviable position of being able to act out the most essential elements of her fantasy without ever having to tell her boyfriend about it. But what if your lover doesn't present his wrists to be tied or his bottom to be spanked or otherwise unwittingly turn the key to your secret thoughts? Should you spill the sexual beans?

The answer is: It depends. While therapists agree that communicating your sexual desires is a good idea, they concede that telling your lover your daydreams could be dangerous—especially if they involve other sex partners. Instead of being turned on by your fantasy of making love to the plumber on the kitchen floor or having a co-worker perform oral sex on you in the office supply closet, he might feel jealous and insulted—even if just a moment before he had insisted that, yes, he really did want to know your innermost thoughts. (Before you get mad, however, think about how *you'd* feel if he disclosed a secret desire for your best girlfriend!)

But there are ways to share—and act out—your fantasies that work and can enhance your sex life together, as long as you proceed with caution—and a little tenderness. Sex therapists suggest playing by the following rules:

1. Talk first, act later. Even if you're not shy about sharing your fantasies, your partner might be. So before you announce you've always dreamed about having sex under the table at a crowded restaurant, attempt to gauge how your lover might feel about trading imaginary sexual scenarios.

Try starting a conversation about the general subject in a nonsexual situation by saying something like: "I was just reading an article on sexual fantasies. People seem to have a lot of fun acting them out. What do you think about that?" If he reacts negatively and starts mumbling about "perverts," it's clearly not safe to reveal your little secret.

But if he smiles and says, "I could get into that," you may be in luck. Ask yourself if you trust him enough, and if you do, go ahead and make reservations at a restaurant with widely spaced tables and long tablecloths. If you think your lover would be receptive, but you're too timid to spell out your secret sex wishes, Joan Elizabeth Lloyd, the author of *Nice Couples Do: How to Turn Your Secret Dreams Into Sensational Sex*, suggests what she calls "bookmarking."

This technique requires no talking, but it's still a powerful communication tool. You simply pick a fantasy you'd like to try acting out from a collection (such as any of Nancy Friday's books, *Penthouse Forum*, or those included in *Nice Couples Do*) and place a bookmark on the appropriate page. Then you leave the book in a place where your lover is sure to find it (on his pillow, perhaps?), and even if you're nowhere within miles, he's certain to get the message. If you're a bit bolder, rent an erotic video with a scene you'd like to try and watch it together. Then just whisper, "That looks like fun" in his ear at the appropriate part, and you probably won't have to do much more.

Whatever method you choose to make your desires known, however, be prepared to compromise when it comes to acting them out. Your man may agree to participate in your restaurant fantasy, and get a kick out of being fondled under the tablecloth while the waiter takes your order. But he may start to feel anxious about being brought to climax while he's waiting for his appetizer—especially if the tablecloth doesn't give full coverage—and need more privacy to take things further.

If that's the case, don't pout and exclaim, "You've ruined it!" Go with the flow and pick a Plan B—make love in the restaurant's one-person-at-a-time ladies room, perhaps, or in your car in the parking lot—that's safer but just as exciting. Or, get the check and dash home if that's the only place he feels completely comfortable.

2. Think it through. Planning ahead for what a fantasy will require, practically and emotionally, will make it run a lot more smoothly. On the practical side, remember the blanket if making love on the beach has always been your dream (sand can be awfully irritating if it gets into the wrong place) or leave your underwear home if you're hoping for a "we-could-get-caught" quickie in a deserted coatroom while everyone else is entranced by the local theater group's production of *Oklahoma!*

You must also plan ahead *emotionally*, which means thinking long and hard about whether you really do want to make it with your mate and a well-hung stranger at the same time. Sex therapists warn that some sexual fantasies just don't work when you bring them out of your mind and into your bedroom. And since there's no way to predict how they'll turn out, it's best to err on the side of caution.

When your fantasy is inside your head, you can play it out perfectly. But once others get involved, it may not unfold the way you'd planned. That's okay if all that happens is that you discover that you really don't like making love on the beach. But actually trying certain kinky things you've dreamed about—a threesome, sex with another woman, or performing so that others can witness every detail—may turn out to be more humiliating than enjoyable. And, if you involve your boyfriend or husband, a fantasy gone wrong could change your relationship *forever*.

In addition, as I mentioned earlier, the secret to your fantasy's incredible arousal power may just be that it *is* a secret, and acting it out could spoil it. I'm not saying *don't* play out your deepest (and perhaps most rewarding) desires, just that you should think through the entire process—and discuss it thoroughly with your lover—before you do.

3. Create a safe word—and stick to it. Before you play out any fantasy—no matter how innocent—you and your partner should agree on a code word which halts the action *immediately*, no questions asked. "No" or "stop" are *not* good choices because so many people say them when they mean just the opposite. Instead pick a word neither one of you is likely to use—or forget—in the heat of passion, and *never* fail to honor your agreement the moment you hear it.

4. Return the favor. Once you share your fantasies, it probably won't be long before your lover chimes in with a request for his favorites. Chances are, they'll be far afield from yours, perhaps so far that you're a little turned off or even disgusted by what he reveals. But, therapists caution that while you're certainly not obligated to act out a fantasy that revolts you, revealing that revulsion to your partner is a big mistake. So, before you say, "The idea of dressing you up in diapers and spanking you like an overgrown baby is the most perverted thing I ever heard!", keep in mind that you may not only be rejecting your lover's fantasy but a big part of his sexuality as well.

As long as playing the punishing mama to his naughty boy won't make you truly uncomfortable, give it a try for his sake—at least once. Or, compromise and agree to the spanking, for example, but not the diapers. No matter what you do, make sure you don't make your lover feel he's bad or disgusting for having sexual desires you don't share. Putting a positive spin on the conversation preserves your partner's self-esteem and keeps the communication channels open between you. That means you'll get to hear his next fantasy, and—who knows?—maybe that one *will* turn you on.

And what are the typical fantasies—and deepest sexual desires—of most males? Get ready for some *big* surprises in the next chapter.

5
WHAT MEN *REALLY* WANT

From the moment Christine walked in the door, she knew something strange was going on. The house should have been empty at that hour of the afternoon, but she heard muffled voices and giggling coming from the living room, and a moment later, moaning.

Her heart beating wildly, Christine, who had left work unusually early that day, took a hesitant step towards the noise, fully expecting to find her husband, Doug, with his arms around another woman. But what she saw when she peeked into the room shocked her even more. The giggling was coming from the television, which pictured two women writhing naked on a bed, their hands and mouths all over each other. Across the room on the couch, Doug sat with his pants off and his legs spread-eagled, one hand pumping furiously on his penis. His head was thrown back, and his eyes were closed.

Christine stood, speechless and transfixed by the scene before her. She was mesmerized by Doug's flying hand until, with a loud groan, his semen shot out—and he opened his eyes and saw her.

For a moment their eyes locked, while Doug's penis deflated in record time and his face got redder and redder. If this had been a male fantasy, the woman in it would simply have licked her lips, smiled a knowing smile, and whispered something like, "Can *I* join the fun? Let's rewind that tape a bit..." Then, acting as though there's nothing sexier than a man satisfying his needs, she'd strip down as her grateful lover watched.

But this was no fantasy. "You pervert! You disgust me!" Christine spit out as she turned and ran up the stairs. Moments later, Doug heard her slam and lock the bedroom door. But he just sat there, so frozen with shame and humiliation, he was unable to even put on his underwear.

Across the room, a man joined the two girls in their frolic, but Doug was no longer watching. He remained glued to the couch, upset with himself for giving in to his urges, and slowly angering at Christine's complete lack of understanding of them. The sexual chasm that had always loomed between him and his wife had just grown much wider—so much so, he wondered if he'd ever be able to bridge it again.

Why He Won't Tell You What Turns Him On

Too many men have used that old cliché, "My wife doesn't understand me" as an excuse to begin an affair. The horrible thing is, it's often all too true—at least *sexually*. We don't understand—and very often, refuse to even tolerate—the fact that, when it comes to sex, men can seem to be a different species, with needs, desires, and responses almost opposite to ours.

"Discovering Doug like that has to be one of the worst experiences of my life," Christine later confided. "He's always been so warm, so loving, so sensitive in bed—I guess it was all a scam. He's not satisfied with me. What he's really wanted all along was to do dirty things with two strange women."

Yes, that's one of Doug's desires (according to many studies, sex with two women is one of the most popular male fantasies, although few men, including Doug, have ever acted it out). But that doesn't make him any less warm, loving, or sensitive. To him, masturbating in front of that X-rated video was no more than a fun way to spend a lazy afternoon, but Christine's horrible reaction made it much more than that.

Fear of just such a reaction is what makes the vast majority of men reluctant to reveal what really turns them on. According to *The McGill Report on Male Sexuality*, "Research data illustrates that fewer than two out of every ten men have disclosed their favorite forms of sex play, their former sex partners, or their sexual fantasies, even to their wives."

That sad statistic is a result of the fact that many women have an extremely rigid definition of what's desirable and proper in the bedroom and how often it should be done. And we expect our lovers to limit themselves to it—even though it may be nearly impossible for a man (no matter how sweet, sensitive, and politically correct he may be in other areas of his life) to conform and still be satisfied.

So what happens? Men are not dopes. If your lover wants to masturbate while watching a porno video—an act he fears you'd label perverted, he'll simply rent a copy of *Two Foxy Vixens* when you're supposed to be out for the afternoon and hope he's not caught.

That's just fine, you may be saying. I'd rather *not* know about his filthy desires. But the truth is that this intolerant attitude is the first brick in a sexual wall many women build, one that prevents them from ever achieving true erotic *and* emotional intimacy with their mates.

You can tear down that wall, even if it's high and sturdy, by studying the mortar of your man's sexual make-up and keeping an open mind to what you find—no matter how shocking. That doesn't mean you should encourage your man to bring home a pair of foxy vixens or that you must join him in watching them cavort on film. But you'll reap great relationship benefits if you manage to expand your definition of acceptable sexuality to include *his* point of view and let him know it's okay to express it with you.

Unfortunately, your man probably won't make it easy for you to discover exactly what his point of view is. Just as with any other emotional issue, "Men don't get much understanding because they have a hard time making a case for themselves, for expressing what's going on with them and how they feel about it," explains Bernie Zilbergeld in his excellent book *The New Male Sexuality*. Afraid of being labeled disgusting or perverted, many men hide their deepest—and most often harmless—desires from us, ashamed because they can't live up to our standards. If you've become aware that something seems to be missing from your sex life, it could be that your man has been holding back sexually because of his fear of being judged.

The goal of this chapter is to help you comprehend the (sometimes immense) differences between your sexuality and your man's and use them to bring you closer together. Simply *trying* to understand where he's coming from is perhaps the single most important part of being a good lover. And that effort will be greatly appreciated—even if you *don't* indulge all his desires!

Inside The Male Sex Machine

Unlike the vast majority of women, men see sex everywhere and in everything, from watching two women kiss each other on the cheek to inserting a key in a lock. And few can ignore the explicitly sexual image without some kind of reaction. That's the reason why, according to the *Kinsey Institute New Report on Sex*, it's normal for the average man to think and fantasize about sex at least once every half-hour, adding up to a whopping *thirty* times a day.

But lest you think your darling is daydreaming when he should be working on his sales report, studies show that most of these libidinous thoughts are brief—lasting only two to thirty seconds—and tend to focus on images of specific body parts or sex acts. The sight of a woman crossing her legs in a meeting might trigger a fantasy of having wild sex on the boardroom table, but fully aware of the inappropriateness of his thought, a man will usually distract himself before he is aroused to erection.

Many men feel embarrassed by the way their X-rated imaginations intrude at the most inopportune moments. "I was in a frenzy at the office over an important project and Amy, a co-worker, and I were working late," recalls Dan, 32, a product manager for a major manufacturer. "The stress was incredible, and when I started to think about how I could relieve it, an image of Amy giving me a blow job popped into my head. It did cheer me up for a moment. But after that, it was more difficult to work with her—not because she turned me on, but because I felt guilty for viewing her as a sex object rather than a colleague."

Like some women, some men feel as though they're committing *mental* adultery when they fantasize. But as Zilbergeld explains, "It's a fact of life that no matter how much a man loves and is turned on by his partner, he will continue to be turned on by and have fantasies about other women."

Jeff, a 30-year-old graphic designer, admits, "Every time I meet a woman, I imagine what she'd look like naked." But he's quick to add, "That doesn't mean I'd do anything even if she were. I love my girlfriend and I would never cheat on her."

Jack, a 26-year-old construction worker, agrees. "I think it's cool to be true, and I wouldn't want to spoil the great relationship I have with my girl. But I'm still attracted to almost every woman who walks by my site. So I use my imagination *instead* of my penis, and it basically satisfies me—or at least takes the edge off my appetite until I get home and can masturbate or have sex with my girlfriend."

In fact, all the men interviewed for this chapter insisted that fantasies help keep them faithful by giving them an innocent way to explore forbidden desires. That was certainly one of the main reasons behind Doug's video choice. "I've always wondered what it would be like to watch two women pleasure each other, but I'd never actually want to *participate* in the act," Doug explains. "First of all, I love Christine too much to ever betray her with one woman, let alone two. But by renting a film, I can indulge my imagination safely just the way she does with those romance novels she's addicted to. She's always drooling over the hunky heroes in those books, but I don't get mad. I wish she understood that."

If there are problems in a relationship, fantasy can become an even more important safety valve. "My wife, who's an investment banker, neglects me emotionally and sexually whenever she goes through a busy period at work," reveals Dale, 26, a teacher. "I really resent it, but nothing I do or say seems to make a difference. Fantasizing about sex with other women—where there are no strings attached and nothing to argue about—seems to help me let off some sexual steam so that I can deal with my real problems with less frustration. I'm not sure why it works, but it does."

What Men Really Want

Men also look at fantasy as a harmless way to continue their sexual adventures after they've made a commitment to remain faithful and to fill gaps in their experience. That's why men often fantasize about women who are totally different than their girlfriends or wives or imagine them engaging in sex acts that they believe their partners would never agree to try.

Just what gaps would your lover most like to fill? Chances are they're on this roster of the typical man's top ten sex acts, in order of preference, compiled by *The Book of Sex Lists*:

1. Fellatio by a woman to orgasm
2. Intercourse with a woman in a variety of positions
3. Sex with two women
4. Caressing a woman's breasts

THE NICE GIRL'S GUIDE TO SENSATIONAL SEX

5. Anal intercourse with a woman
6. Simultaneous oral sex
7. Performing mild sadomasochistic acts on a woman
8. Being masturbated by a woman
9. Performing cunnilingus
10. Masturbation

You might not be willing to perform some of the acts on this list—or have them performed on you—no matter how much your partner begs. Nor should you have to (although you'll find instructions for several of them later in this book). But there are things you *should* be willing to do for your man—even if they seem silly, unnecessary, or perhaps go against feminist teachings.

Most men insist they don't need or even want a Sharon Stone lookalike for a lover. But they all mention the same factors that can magically turn an ordinary woman into a sex goddess *or* a wicked witch with whom their first bedroom encounter is likely to be the last. Here are twelve revealing tips from the men themselves on how to turn them on—and off. And not one of them is beyond the reach of *any* woman.

Sex Goddess Secrets

1. Present A Clean, Attractive Package.

When passion is on the agenda, think: less is more, especially where perfume, makeup, and hair products are concerned. Men are biologically programmed to be aroused by a woman's natural smells. Strange as it may seem, a whiff of your armpit may drive him crazy with desire, and scent of your vagina certainly will (one of the reasons men love to perform oral sex on their partners). But your armpits, your vagina, your breath, your entire body must be scrupulously clean in order to inspire this ardor—although not *sanitized* with strong deodorants and douches, which one man said made his lover smell like "a hospital." (If you must douche, use the old-fashioned vinegar and water formula.) Go easy on the perfume as well; the idea is to let your own sweet scent come through.

In addition, use a light hand on your blush brush. Ben, a 32-year-old police detective, says he doesn't mind getting a little lipstick on his face or collar. "I find it kind of sexy. But I don't like seeing a lot of makeup on a woman up close. It looks artificial and slutty."

Jeff, the graphic designer, is even more adamant that his lovers be bare-faced. "I remember making love once after a party," he explains. "My date had been really dressed up and she looked great. But as soon as she began to sweat a little during sex, her makeup started smearing. Before I knew it, some of the yucky stuff had rubbed off on me and she looked a mess. She had these black rings under her eyes and her lipstick was all over the place. I was too embarrassed to ask her to wash her face, but I never took her out again."

Of course, unless you have perfect skin, the idea of facing a man without your usual makeup can be a bit daunting. If you don't have the courage—or naturally long, lush lashes—at least wear products that won't smudge or sweat off: gel blush, lip pencil (instead of lipstick), liquid eye liner, and truly waterproof mascara (or the regular kind sealed with two coats of colorless mascara; let each coat dry completely before applying the next).

Sticky and stiff hair styling products also get bad press from men. "I want to be able to run my hands through lots of soft hair," says Kenneth, 29, a real estate broker, "not stuff that's hard as a rock with hairspray or so full of mousse and gunk that my hand gets stuck." So if a strong wind wouldn't ruffle your mane, you may want to rethink your hair style.

If you like nail polish, make sure it's near perfect—or don't wear it at all. No man wants to look down at the hand that's caressing his thigh and see chipped, peeling polish and ragged cuticles. And, although men are never asked their opinion of the long nails many women work so hard to achieve, few really like them. "They look nice," says Ben. "But they get in the way of making love. I've been scratched in some delicate places a few times—and that's a definite turn-off."

One last note: keep jewelry to a *bare* minimum. You may feel naked without your charm bracelet and your ID necklace, but when you're making love, that's the idea. Long earrings, necklaces, and bracelets can be jangly and distracting, even downright painful, as one man found out when his girlfriend (who was in the female superior position) leaned down to kiss him and bopped him hard in the face with a rather large pendant instead. "It made a little cut on the tip of my nose and I started bleeding," he recalls. "I didn't feel much like making love after that."

2. Keep Your Body Anxiety Under Wraps.

Women love to commiserate with others about their flabby thighs, saggy breasts, those few extra pounds around their tummies. Trouble is, these self-deprecating comments should be saved for your girlfriends (who can really appreciate them) and never made in front of a man, least of all one who is feeling quite excited by the body you swear you "despise." If you see an erection coming your way, you can take it for granted that the man who owns it either hasn't noticed the cellulite on your derriere—or he simply doesn't care. But point out "the amazing ripple effect" when you rub your thighs together, and you just might convince him that your bod is as undesirable as you claim.

So when your lover whispers, "You have such a pretty body," don't disagree and say something dopey like "Oh, no. I'm way too fat." He believes it—you should too. Forget the flab and accept the compliment. If being totally nude makes you nervous, cover up your worst spots with some enticing lingerie. And if you absolutely must say something to allay your anxiety, tell your lover, "I hope you like my body as must as I like yours." And leave it at that.

3. DON'T PRAISE—OR PUT DOWN— YOUR PREVIOUS LOVERS.

Though he's probably guessed you're not a 32-year-old virgin, it's never a good idea to remind him that some other guy (or maybe *many* guys) discovered your luscious curves first. But the main reason you should never tell tales (good or bad) about another man's technique is that it can put undue pressure on your present lover.

"I had been dating Robyn for a few weeks and really started to fall for her," Peter, 27, reveals. "The first time we slept together, I was incredibly excited—until she started comparing me to other men she'd had. When she said, 'Oh, you're so much bigger than I'm used to,' I was sort of pleased. But then she told me her last lover had always come too fast for her, and the pressure was on. I remember thinking of baseball stats, doing all sorts of equations in my head just so I'd be sure to last longer than the other guy had. Needless to say, I didn't enjoy it very much."

Men are even less forgiving if the comparison is *unfavorable*. "It was our second date, and I'd had a terrific time with Mara," Don, a restaurant manager, recalls. "She seemed so smart and sophisticated. But I'd had a little too much to drink, and when it came time for the main event, I just couldn't get an erection, even though I was dying to make love to her.

"She spent a few minutes massaging my penis, trying hard to make me hard, but nothing worked. I was really embarrassed, but I appreciated her efforts—until she stopped and blurted out, 'What's wrong with you? My last lover never had this problem!'

"I was so humiliated, I wanted to cry. And so angry, I wanted to kick her out of bed," Don says, the hurt still in his voice. "I didn't do either one, but I never asked her out again."

4. INSPIRE TRUST.

In the age of AIDS, knowing that you're disease-free is obviously (or at least should be) important to your lover. But your man is also seeking *emotional* safety when he enters your arms. He needs to know from your words, gestures, and general attitude that you could handle it—and help him handle it—if he lost his erection and that you won't be disgusted if he wants to try something new, perhaps even a bit kinky. He needs to know he can trust you with his sexual ego, even if it's rather fragile (and almost all of them *are*).

"I've always been obsessed with women's backsides, and for a long time, I've fantasized about having anal sex. But I was never brave enough to ask a lover," says Ken, the lawyer who's dating Kelly, the legal secretary. "But Kelly made me feel so comfortable, so loved, that one night I gathered my courage and mumbled something about wanting to try sex 'back there.'

"There was this long moment of silence when I feared I had really turned her off. But then she turned to me and said that she didn't think she'd enjoy anal sex, but that she was willing to try something else new—like being spanked a little. It wasn't exactly what I wanted, but it was something fun for us to do that allowed me to play with her ass. A few light taps, and we were both turned on. And the fact that she was so nonjudgmental made me love her even more."

5. Center Your Attention On *Him*.

I disagree with that old saying: familiarity breeds contempt. What it really breeds in many long-term relationships is a lack of complete concentration on your partner. No longer are you enchantingly, totally engrossed with him, willing to stare into his eyes and drink in his words for hours on end. Instead, just about anything from *Wheel of Fortune* to washing out your pantyhose can steal away your time together—including time for sex.

According to Sidney Biddle Barrows, the infamous former Mayflower Madam, one of the main reasons men use call girls is to have a woman's *undivided* attention. "When a man goes to a call girl, she's completely there for him," Barrows explains in a highly informative class she gives for New York City's Learning Annex called "Just Between Us Girls." "She's not doing the laundry or answering the phone." In addition, the conversation is light, not focused on the fact that the roof has to be fixed or the bills have to be paid the way it is at home. "Often, the sexual part is over in fifteen minutes, sometimes *five*," says Barrows, "but the client continues to pay for the girl's time, just so they can cuddle and *talk*."

Obviously, the roof does have to be fixed and the bills do have to be taken care of, and you can't ignore them. But you don't need to remain bogged down in the details of daily life during every minute you're home—especially in the bedroom. As Barrows suggests, take the time just to be together. Make your bed a sacred place of fun and shut out the rest of the world (yes, even your kids!).

Unfortunately, many women make a bad habit of bringing up problems at bedtime (few men are guilty of this), increasing the tension when both partners need to reduce it. So, even if you're not having sex, ban all talk of bills, social obligations, childcare problems, and the like from the moment you hit the sheets each night. Let your man know he's important enough to warrant your *complete* attention, at least for a little while. That leaky roof isn't going anywhere, but your relationship might spring a few holes if you're not careful.

6. Make The First Move— At Least Sometimes.

Gene, 29, an account executive for a large advertising firm, has been struggling to keep his biggest client, a food manufacturer who is threatening to jump to another agency and put Gene's job in jeopardy. Gene used to love coming to the office, but now every day brings make-or-break decisions and the stress is definitely getting to him. His girlfriend, Laura, has been supportive—but not in the way he'd most appreciate. "Our sex life has always been my responsibility," Gene says. "Most of the time, I'm content to make the first move. But I've noticed that if I don't, we simply never make love, and that bothers me. Just once, I wish she'd show me that she *does* desire me by initiating sex."

From childhood, men are conditioned to be the romantic and sexual aggressors, to ask for a date, to press for that first kiss, undo a woman's bra, lead her to bed. A man loves being a seducer when a woman returns his kisses with equal passion. But there's always the risk that he'll try to reach under her sweater and find a hand firmly blocking his progress, that he'll put his ego on the line and be painfully rebuffed. It's a difficult prospect to face, and creates a constant pressure women find hard to understand.

And this pressure may not abate even in an established relationship as long as the woman continues to assume the man will always be the one to initiate sex. "I always thought one of the nice things about having a steady girlfriend would be that I'd no longer have to constantly risk rejection," Gene explains. "But I was wrong. Since I'm always the one to start things off, I still risk rejection each night—and I hate it."

Even though it may *seem* that Gene's girlfriend has the advantage here, this pattern is unfair to her as well, because when a woman feels she must always wait for the man to take the initiative, it robs her of the opportunity to express her own desire to make love.

But if you make the first move, it allows your lover to relax and escape, at least sometimes, the awful pressure of always being in charge of sex. It also means you find the dear boy too dreamy to resist, even if you've both had a hard day at work—and I don't need to tell you what an ego boost that is!

7. Let There Be Light.

The quickest way to a man's heart may be through his stomach, but the quickest way to his penis is definitely through his eyes. Unlike women, men are highly aroused by visual stimuli (thus the popularity of porn films and "dirty" magazines), and the more they see, the more they're turned on. Many, I'm sure, would love to have sex under a spotlight so that they could drink in every detail of their lover's body, the way their penis looks thrusting in and out of her vagina or mouth, the way their hand looks caressing her breasts.

That's why the darkened room that women often prefer when making love can be a disappointment, even a hindrance if their man has trouble achieving an erection. So put your shyness aside and leave one light on (or at least several candles) if you can. Or surprise him with a special treat:

Start making love in a dark room, then use a small flashlight to illuminate your hot spots!

8. CREATE ADVENTURE.

"Many prostitutes and call girls report that a significant portion of their clientele consists of happily married men who come to them only for some variety," claims Zilbergeld. "And men are more likely than women to have affairs, and not necessarily because something is lacking at home, except for a variety of partners."

Does this mean you're doomed to have a lover who strays? Not necessarily—as long as you provide the variety of partners (that is, sexual adventures) he craves. Being an enticing and creative enchantress involves more than letting him do it to you doggie-style every once in a while, however. Use your imagination. Think of unusual locations for a romantic tryst. Is he a golf fanatic? Try the eighteenth hole one night when the links are deserted—it's sure to improve his game. A good sense of timing also counts. For example, wake him up a little early with a deliciously *slow* blow job. He'll be chipper all day!

You can also add an exciting sense of newness to your next encounter by playing a few pretend games. Consider donning a French maid costume and a long blonde wig. Or try using scented massage oils all over his body, or silky scarves for tying wrists and ankles (no, you don't have to use all of the above at once). Ruth Dickson, the author of *Married Men Make the Best Lovers*, suggests making love in a bathtub that's been filled with Jello! Okay, so maybe you'd rather stick to bubble bath, but you get the idea.

This is not to say you must transform your bedroom into a three-ring bordello each and every night. But it's never a bad idea to break out of what might have become a boring bedtime-only routine, and keep him so thoroughly satisfied, he won't have the energy—or the inclination—to look elsewhere. Another major benefit: Inspired by your wild imaginings, he's likely to spring some sizzling scenarios on you. (See Chapter Seven to expand your erotic repertoire even further.)

9. Pursue Your Own Pleasure.

A woman who can be counted on to help achieve her own orgasm is always a highly rated lover. Many surveys have found that, far from ignoring their partners' pleasure, most men are so focused on it that they can't enjoy themselves unless they're sure their lovers are too. Perhaps that's because a man never feels more sexy, more powerful, more turned on than when he knows he's turning *you* on.

The problem is, how much—or little—a woman is aroused is often far from obvious to him. "I'll be in the middle of intercourse and suddenly realize that what I'm doing just isn't working for my lover," says Marco, 39, and newly divorced. "But when I ask what I could do that would feel better, women always say, 'Oh, what you're doing feels just fine.' It's very aggravating and it makes me feel stupid, like I should know how to make her come, but I can't figure it out."

Of course, his partner probably feels just as frustrated as he gets closer and closer to climax and she's left behind. But the situation doesn't have to end in disappointment, as Gretta, a 26-year-old secretary joyously discovered. Foreplay with her boyfriend Todd would leave her bubbling with passion, but as soon as they began intercourse, her excitement level would drop because her clitoris was no longer getting the stimulation it needed.

Todd sensed something was wrong and pressed Gretta to reveal it, "but somehow I was just too shy to tell him. Then, one night I was feeling so frustrated, I literally took the matter into my own hands." As Todd was about to enter her, Gretta grabbed his penis and started rubbing her clitoris with it, using him like a human vibrator to pleasure herself.

"I couldn't believe what I was doing, but I couldn't stop either—I just had to climax. When I opened my eyes, Todd was smiling. He loved it! He told me there's nothing sexier than a woman going after an orgasm, and that he'd never been so aroused. Now, I turn on my 'vibrator' whenever I need it. I don't have to suffer in silence—and neither does he."

10. Don't Take Sex Too Seriously.

Men look at sex as a form of fabulous recreation, and it would benefit many women if they were able to take this view too. Yes, it's an important means of expressing love for your partner, but it's also a great way to reduce stress, forget about the rest of the world, just kick back and have fun.

If you take sex too seriously, you rob your man—and yourself—of the playful element that's so integral to full, relaxed pleasure. In addition, you're going to need your sense of humor when things go wrong—his erection misses your vagina, he pulls your hair by mistake, you fart (whoops!)

at an inopportune moment—or they'll go even wronger. But learn to laugh off these sexual bloopers and you and he will have a much better time.

So try to keep the mood light and frisky, and don't be afraid to make a joke or two. According to Graham Masterton, author of *How to Drive Your Man Wild in Bed*, only one subject should be taboo: your lover's limp penis. "Joke about it when it's stiff, but never when it's dangly."

11. BE ENTHUSIASTIC.

"The women of male fantasies are always young, sexually insatiable, readily available, unashamedly exposed, and very experienced sexually," says Dr. Miriam Stoppard, author of *The Magic of Sex*. "If they were able to express any preferences, they would be delighted with whatever a man did to them, and they would be begging for more."

But in real life, a man often gets indifference instead of delight. Many women, especially once they're certain of a man's affections, seem to put sex on the back burner over a *very low* flame. Others feel it's not "nice" to show too great a libidinous interest or move around too much in bed. So they just lie there and let love be made *to* them, making their man feel rejected, dirty, embarrassed, *wrong* for wanting and enjoying sex. Still others consider sex pleasant, but basically unimportant and treat it that way.

Well, that's certainly not the way your man feels! In a major survey of four thousand American men in *Beyond the Male Myth* by Anthony Pietropinto and Jacqueline Simmenauer, 61 percent rated sex as "very important" and an additional 20 percent called it "life's major pleasure." Even more revealing, only 2 percent said "other things matter more." So it's no wonder that when these same men were polled for the biggest turn-off in bed, a whopping 59 percent picked a partner's *unresponsiveness*.

In general, sex paves the way to greater emotional intimacy. When a man loves you, he uses sex to express that love and forge a deeper connection between you—something he may not be able to do in words. If you fail to respond to this reaching out, he's likely to feel hurt, confused, terribly unloved. He may also be more than a little angry, and distance himself even further from you. But since it's a rare man who voices these problems, you may never know until your relationship is already in deep jeopardy.

Less than a year after Joelle and Rick started dating, he noticed her interest in sex seemed to be flagging. "She never took the initiative anymore, and often she'd brush me off with the slightest excuse," Rick, a 28-year-old film editor, reveals. "When we were in bed together, I could tell she was just going through the motions. She wasn't enthusiastic at all. I might as well have been masturbating."

Ironically, the couple's sexual troubles began soon after Rick had proposed marriage, and Joelle, 27, a sound engineer, had accepted. Getting engaged had been a major goal of Joelle's, and she had done everything she could to entice Rick—including faking many hip-shaking orgasms each time they made love. In fact, she didn't enjoy sex with Rick much at all, but never sought his help in remedying the situation. Instead, her goal accomplished, she relaxed and faked less and less frequently.

Rick noticed the change immediately, and doubled his sexual efforts—only to be increasingly disturbed when they obviously didn't work the way they once had. It wasn't long after that Rick began to doubt that he'd chosen the right fiancée. "I adore Joelle," he says. "But I looked ahead and saw a bleak sexual future, where I would always be feeling guilty for forcing her to have sex just to satisfy my 'piggy' needs. I couldn't figure out what had gone wrong, and it made me very sad and confused."

One night, Joelle was reaching the end of a Steven King novel when Rick tried to interest her in making love, taking the book out of her hands and covering her face with kisses. Joelle allowed herself to be led into bed, but angry that her reading had been interrupted, she lay passively below Rick, making no move or sound.

For about ten minutes, Rick kissed and touched her with little response. "Then suddenly, something in me just snapped," recalls Rick. "I yelled, 'What's wrong with you? Are you asleep? Why don't I turn you on the way I used to? I can't go on like this!' All my anger and confusion poured out."

Faced with continuing to fake wild orgasms for the rest of her life or losing her fiancé, Joelle decided to come clean. "She started to cry and admitted that she'd never had an orgasm with me or any other man, and was afraid that she couldn't. At first, I was even angrier that she'd lied to me, but when she said she wanted to stop faking and try to have a real orgasm with me, that she wanted us to work on it together, my heart melted. Now she recognizes how important it is for me to feel she's enjoying herself in bed, and I'm going to do my best to make sure she *really* does."

Just as it's ill-mannered not to compliment a cook on a meal he or she has slaved over, it's rude not to respond when a man is trying his damndest to please you in bed. But even more important, being a good lover is central to most men's sense of desirability and self-worth. While you're certainly not obligated to make love each time he asks or thrash around the bed in the throes of a bogus orgasm, a general lack of enthusiasm on your part may eventually make your lover question his self-worth—and resent you for it (just think how you'd feel about yourself if he looked bored at the prospect of yet another tumble with you).

But you can remedy the situation before it gets out of hand by being an active, *eager* partner, and using this book to learn how to enjoy yourself in bed (if you don't already) so there's no need for phony passion. You owe it to *both* of you!

12. DON'T BE STINGY WITH COMPLIMENTS.

Years of looking at superslim models in fashion magazines have certainly taken their toll on the average woman's body image. But men have always seemed immune to such insecurity, more likely to think, "Hey, my body's still in pretty good shape," even when a pot belly has started to hang over their jeans. Several surveys taken in the early 1980s demonstrated that, unlike their mates, most men thought they were *more* attractive than they actually were.

Well, all that's changed slowly over the last decade ever since advertisers (most notably Calvin Klein) started using gorgeous—and often quite

THE NICE GIRL'S GUIDE TO SENSATIONAL SEX   153

bare—male bodies to sell their products. As Jeff, the graphic designer, put it, "Everywhere I go, I see pictures of almost naked men with killer arms, sculpted chests, washboard stomachs—and I see my girlfriend looking at them with lust in her eyes. The first time she saw a billboard with Marky Mark sporting skintight Calvin Klein skivvies and a rather obvious bulge, she almost slammed the car into the back of a bus. That was the day I decided to join a gym."

Jeff isn't the only one feeling insecure about his physical attractiveness, and many men are putting their money where their anxiety is. Plastic surgeons report that business is up as more men than ever before crowd in for pectoral (chest) implants, calf implants, and liposuction—all in the hopes of looking more virile to us. Some surgeons, such as Dr. Brian Novack in Los Angeles, have even been performing a relatively new procedure called PABFAT in which fat from another part of the body is transplanted into the penis, increasing its girth by as much as 30 percent.

Why do they care so much? "There is hardly a man who does not need to feel loved, admired, and physically cherished if he is to experience the true depths of sexual pleasure with his partner," says Dr. Miriam Stoppard. So the next time your man bares his bod to you, find something nice to say about it! Ignore the love handles and compliment his large hairy chest or cute little butt with complete sincerity. Pick a favorite body part and praise it often.

Of course, the body part your lover most wants you to like is his penis. But on one level, some women are actually a little afraid of erections—and show that fear or distaste by handling their lover's equipment as if it were a small, rabid animal that bites. And most men will not only be turned off by this attitude, but take personal offense to it as well.

It's human nature to fear what you don't know—and a penis is no exception. But you can learn to handle your man's most cherished possession with comfortable confidence if you'll only take the time to learn how it works, how to nurture your man's erection, and *guarantee* his extreme pleasure. You'll find everything you'll ever want—or need—to know about that finicky, fickle, sometimes awe-inspiring instrument in the next chapter.

6
LOVE HIM, LOVE HIS PENIS

What makes the perfect penis? Perhaps not surprisingly, men and women often answer this question differently. "The bigger, the better" is the motto most men live—and worry—by. As psychologist Bernie Zilbergeld puts it in his book *The New Male Sexuality*, "In [male] fantasyland, penises come in only three sizes—large, gigantic, and so big you can barely get them through the door."

Yet in a recent *Cosmo* Sex Survey, when several thousand women were asked to name the essential elements of great sex, a big penis was *last* on the list, preceded by passion, tenderness, doing new things, the man's orgasm, the woman's orgasm, and a man's staying power, in that order.

Of course, some women are so *psychologically* excited by the sight of monstrous member that they have a hard time settling for something smaller. But the truth is that the length of your partner's penis has about as much to do with your *physical* pleasure—or his—as the length of his nose.

A woman's vagina contracts and expands to accommodate almost any object that finds its way into it from a tampon to a baby's head during birth. And since the outer third (about 1½ inches) of the canal is the only part that's truly responsive to stimulation, it's well within the reach of even a small penis, let alone the average six- to seven-inch erection. (If his equipment seems small on first inspection and size does truly matter to you, don't despair. As a rule, the smaller the penis, the proportionately larger the erection. Numerous studies by Masters and Johnson found that soft penises measuring 3 to 3½ inches *doubled* in size when erect, while those 4 to 4¾ inches long when soft grew only an additional 30 percent.) If anything, some women report that a thicker penis (they range from around 2.3 to 4.7 inches in circumference) makes them feel "fuller."

But in general, although some well-hung gents would love to rest on their larger-than-average laurels, there's much truth in that old adage: "It's not what you've got, but how you *use* it that counts."

Making Friends With His Favorite Body Part

No matter what his natural endowment, he'll be more inspired to make the most of it if you look upon his penis as a treasured chum. Though most men won't admit it, they often think of their pride and joy as a separate and sometimes uncooperative individual, and will be amazed at your incredible insight if you treat it as such. Some even give their penises nicknames. If your lover hasn't, go ahead and bestow one (Alexander the Great, Warrior of Love, Big Bad John?) one night when you're goofing around. He may *say* it's silly, but he'll be pleased you're paying it the tribute he hopes it deserves.

But becoming pals with his penis means more

THE NICE GIRL'S GUIDE TO SENSATIONAL SEX 157

than giving it a pet name. As you'll see, it pays to know your new playmate inside *and* out!

A Penis Primer

Though we've all seen a penis in action, you may not know what goes on behind the sexual scenes *inside* a man's body. Despite the emphasis your lover places on this treasured private part, his brain (like yours) is really his primary sexual organ. When his brain is aroused, it sends messages down his spinal cord to increase the blood flow to the spongy tissues which make up his penis and stop the flow out, which causes an erection. (Although an erection is sometimes called a boner, the penis has no bone nor striated muscle tissue, the kind that can be enlarged with exercise—sorry, boys!)

Until just before orgasm, anything—from the thought that he's not pleasing you to a drop in the stimulation he needs to please him—can cause his erection to droop, even deflate completely. But if he gets to the brink of orgasm, neither rain, sleet, nor snow could keep him from climaxing.

You can tell he's reached the point of no return when his breathing quickens, his thighs tense, and his testicles draw up into his body. The head of his penis may also darken in color and swell, and a few drops of pre-ejaculatory fluid seep out of the slit.

During orgasm, a man's urethra contracts four or five times in as many seconds, forcing his semen to shoot out (if it just sort of dribbles instead, that's perfectly normal too). The more sex he's had recently, the less semen he'll ejaculate. But don't use this as an iron-clad test of his fidelity, since some men just produce a lower volume.

Although most men experience orgasm and ejaculation as one event, some sex researchers insist that it's possible to enjoy one *without* the other. They take the view that orgasm is simply a sudden, pleasurable release of tension *anywhere* in the body. As a result, they hypothesize that men, like women, can experience multiple orgasms before ejaculating. According to Dr. Miriam Stoppard, author of *The Magic of Sex*, "With practice and learned control, many men can extend their sexual cycles and enjoy several mini orgasms before a final climax."

Sounds like wishful thinking to me. But one thing is certain: after ejaculating, all men go through what's called a refractory period during which they're unable to get another erection. While it lasts just a few minutes (if that) during adolescence, a penis needs an increasing amount of nap time as it gets older. A 20-year-old's refractory period lasts only about ten minutes, but that may double—or even triple—by the time a man hits forty. And a 50-year-old's penis will almost always need a full day's rest before it can reach a second erection. So do be patient!

Finding Your Way Around

Where and how your lover likes to be touched depends upon his individual preferences, but many men are so focused on their penises they don't even realize how good it feels to have their earlobes nibbled, their buttocks caressed, their nipples licked (his breasts might actually be *more* responsive than yours!).

So show him what he's missed out on with his other lovers—keep your hands and mouth moving, introduce a new type of touch and take pleasure in his reaction, then encourage him to do the same for you. Take the time to appreciate all his nooks and crannies, the places where his skin is rough, hairy, or baby smooth. Make his body your playground and neither one of you will ever be bored in bed again. He has all *sorts* of toys that are fun to try out.

Don't ignore his penis for too long, however. Here, too, there is uncharted territory to explore. A man may think he knows every possible way to pleasure himself, but introduce him to an exciting new caress or rhythm, and he'll be in grateful awe of your sexual artistry.

If you've never examined a penis, tell your lover you'd like to study his, then go down for a closer look. While the whole shaft is deliciously sensitive, the mushroom-shaped head (also called the glans) is particularly blessed with an abundance of nerve endings. Other hot spots include: the frenulum (that tiny triangular patch of flesh where the head meets the shaft—definitely worth searching for), the testicles (unless he's too ticklish to enjoy being touched there), and the small stretch of skin that lies behind his balls, between the base of the penis and the anus.

Of course, your man's hottest spot of all is his brain. Take the time to excite him *mentally* (whisper the naughty thing you plan to do to him next, for example, encourage him to admire the way his penis looks thrusting in and out of you, or tell him how hard and big he feels), and his imagination will help fill in any gaps in your technique.

What You Can Learn From The Way He Masturbates

You can pick up a lot of pointers on pleasing a man this way, so if your lover volunteers to demonstrate, don't turn him down out of prudishness or embarrassment. Like women, men have many different ways of self-pleasuring. Some start stroking light and slow, while the hands of others are a blur right from the beginning. But most use lotion, oil, or spit (in a pinch) to make their fingers glide more smoothly, and move up and down the entire shaft, including, but not focusing, on the ultra-sensitive head.

As their climax approaches, even the slow strokers get up to speed and move their hands as rapidly as possible—until ejaculation, when most men slow down or stop completely, since right after orgasm, the tip of the penis is so sensitive that the slightest touch can be *painful*. Because most women do like stimulation to continue all the way through orgasm, many don't realize that their enthusiastic pumping or thrusting (during and after his climax) is overkill, and their partners are too embarrassed to tell them. So it's best to observe a hands-off policy after his orgasm until your lover lets you know otherwise.

Though you may think masturbation is something he can—and should—do for himself, masturbating your man can be a wonderful addition to your repertoire that you can use when one or both of you are tired or as an appetizer which will get his first (usually quickest) orgasm out of the way and increase his staying power for later intercourse.

It's a skill worth perfecting. As *Joy of Sex* author

THE NICE GIRL'S GUIDE TO SENSATIONAL SEX

Alex Comfort writes, "A woman who knows how to masturbate a man—subtly, unhurriedly, and mercilessly—will almost always make a superlative partner."

Even if you've never made love in this way before, it's easy to turn your hands into instruments of exquisite pleasure. Here's how: Use one hand to hold his penis steady at the bottom or to fondle his testicles. Then make a circle with your thumb and index finger or use your whole hand to grip him and slide up and down. Hand lotion or even vegetable oil will speed you along, but if you're planning to allow him inside you afterwards, stick to a water-based lubricant (see page 199 for some suggestions), which won't irritate your vagina.

When men masturbate, many bring themselves to climax as quickly as possible (a leftover from the days when they were always scared of being caught). But your goal is a *slow* buildup of sensation in order to prolong the pleasure. So the first few times your lover approaches orgasm (ask him to warn you if you can't tell for sure), ease up on the speed and intensity of your stimulation, or even stop completely until he calms down a *bit* (don't pause too long, however, or you'll have an angry man on your hands). The idea is to keep him dangling on the edge of ecstasy before you finally supply him with the speedy strokes he needs to take the plunge straight into an incredible orgasm.

There's nothing like masturbating a man (except perhaps fellating him—see page 163) to increase a woman's sexual confidence. So don't just pump him halfheartedly—put some soul and creativity into it (experiment with fast and slow strokes, short and long, soft and hard, as well as rolling his penis between your palms, squeezing it gently).

Revel in the control you have over his climax and make the most of it. If you're really good at this sort of sexual "torture," he may be unable to take it unless you tie him down!

HIS G-SPOT

Men do have one, and as usual, it's a lot easier to find theirs than ours. His G-spot is an internal gland called the prostate (which produces some of the fluid that sperm swim in) and can be found by putting your thumb into his anus and pressing against the front wall.

"Ugh! No way!" may be your first reaction. But consider this: unless he's constipated, your finger won't touch anything but skin—the same stuff that covers the rest of his body. And massaging that prostate will produce such incredibly intense pleasure (many men become erect and climax by G-spot stimulation alone) that you'll instantly be elevated to sex goddess status.

How to find it: Lubricate your thumb or index finger with K-Y Jelly (don't try this with long nails!), then insert your finger very slowly and leave it in place for a moment without moving (it's going to feel a little funny for him too). Then feel around *gently* until you find the prostate—a little lump about the size of a walnut on the wall nearest his stomach. Massaging it or stroking it in the downward direction should make him feel sublime. If you really want to make him your sex slave, perform fellatio at the same time.

Just one caution: always wash your hands thoroughly afterwards—especially *before* touching your vagina. Bacteria that is harmless in the rectum can wreak havoc in your genitals.

Oral Sex: The Blow-by-Blow Basics

When I was doing research for this chapter, I asked dozens of men to name the act at the top of their sexual wish list. "A really great blow job," replied Robert, a 28-year-old accountant, with a dreamy look in his eyes. His response was echoed by the rest, almost without exception. And if you don't believe me, studies back up my findings. According to Pepper Schwartz and Philip Blumstein, the authors of *American Couples*, "Heterosexual men who receive oral sex are happier with their sex lives and with their relationships in general."

The combination of concentrated stimulation, a bird's-eye view (not possible in most intercourse positions), and the complete lack of pressure to perform gives fellatio an irresistible erotic kick for almost every man alive. So if your man hasn't asked you to "go down on him," it's probably *not* because it doesn't have immense appeal to him, but because he's afraid it will have absolutely none for you.

That may be so (although I do hope to change your mind). Perhaps you've even told him as much in words or resistant gestures. Many women find the thought of putting a penis in their mouths repugnant because they view it as a dirty excretory organ. But the two of you can make sure his penis is completely clean before it ever approaches your sweet lips by incorporating a shower or even a playful little sponge bath into your foreplay (in any case, urine is 100 percent bacteria-free).

In addition, if a woman has had the awful experience of a lover (usually a very young or casual one) holding her head and forcing his manhood down her throat, oblivious to her pain and gagging, she too may fear fellatio. But if a man loves you, putting his penis in your mouth won't turn him into a raging beast. He'll remain the same gentle lover during fellatio that he's always been, albeit a happier one. And there are many ways to completely prevent gagging, choking, or *any discomfort at all*.

In addition, being adept at the oral arts comes in handy for those times you feel like having sex, but not intercourse, such as when you're menstruating, want to have more control over your orgasm (you can masturbate while performing fellatio—either with or *without* his knowledge), or if you simply forgot (oops!) that darned diaphragm or your other birth control.

So at least read this section and try to keep an open mind. If you push aside your misgivings long enough to try it, you may find you actually like fellatio, or, at the very least, get an ego-gratifying boost from your lover's enthusiastic reaction. As one woman put it, "Performing oral sex is a true power trip for me. It's a gift of pure pleasure I give my lover when he's been an especially good boy—and he's always *wildly* grateful!"

Other women hesitate to navigate down below because they're afraid they'll do it "wrong." If that's the only thing that's stopping you, consider this: When men are asked what makes a stellar blow job, they *never* mention a woman's technique. Instead, it's her obvious enthusiasm that makes all the difference between a mind-blowing experience and just a blowing one.

That's one of the reasons that the first rule of

THE NICE GIRL'S GUIDE TO SENSATIONAL SEX 165

good oral sex is: Let him see you do it. Men are much more visually oriented than women, and the sight of your lips closing around his penis (keep at least one light on!) will have a powerful erotic impact. Let him see you slowly lick those lips first in sincere anticipation, and he'll be halfway to climax from the thought of how much you want him.

The more you excite your man visually (and therefore mentally), the less work you'll have to do in order to bring him to orgasm. That's why it's best (for him) if he lies down and you kneel on one side, although kneeling in front of him while he sits on a chair or the bed also allows him a clear view.

If you've never performed fellatio before, start by giving him your most sultry look, and—without breaking eye contact, if possible—take the head of his penis (only the first inch or so) into your mouth *slowly*, before letting it pop back out again. Then, gripping the shaft at its base to hold it steady (it will also allow you to control the depth of his thrusts), leisurely lick his penis like an ice cream cone, swirling your tongue around the head in order to get him good and wet.

At this point, cover your teeth with your lips and take the head of his penis into your mouth, sucking it like a lollipop. Most women feel comfortable sucking just the head and stimulating the shaft with their hands, licking up and down its length occasionally to lubricate it. You can try relaxing your throat muscles and taking his whole penis into your mouth, but few women are able to do this without gagging, so don't feel guilty if you can't (if he's rude enough to demand you "deep throat" him, point out that you'd never ask him to do something that would make *him* gag).

As with any type of lovemaking, you'll need to experiment to see what sorts of movements and rhythms most excite your darling, then change them often to keep him in suspense. Speeding up, and then slowing down when you feel his shaft suddenly increase in hardness (a possible indication that he's about to climax) will keep him ecstatically teetering on the brink of orgasm—and sanity—until you deign to put him out of that marvelous misery.

READY, SET, SWALLOW?

While some men don't care whether you gulp down their semen, others get an erotic kick out of it and may even become quite pouty if you refuse (how could you not love every part of him?). Some women do adore the taste and sensation of their lover's ejaculation (and at a measly five to nine calories a shot, even the most stringent dieters need not worry. Semen even contains a bit of calcium, along with 120 million to 600 million sperm per teaspoon!). And as "J," the author of *The Sensuous Woman*, writes, "Mouth/penis orgasm gives you the opportunity to *really* feel and share the explosion of his coming to climax (you just don't have the sensitivity in the vagina) and this can be a thrilling experience for a woman."

But for most women, swallowing is one thrill they'd just as soon pass up. To prevent being put in an uncomfortable position, tell your lover you'd rather not have him climax in your mouth *before* you start, so you'll both know what to expect at the crucial point.

THE SECRET NO-SWALLOW TECHNIQUE

Still, if you sense he might be put off by your reluctance—or if you'd just rather not bring the subject up, there is an alternative. Sydney Biddle Barrows, the former Mayflower Madam, created what she calls her Secret No-Swallow Technique for the high-class call girls of the service she once ran in New York City. The clients never knew the girls didn't swallow—and neither will your partner.

Here's her technique, which Barrows passes on to women around the country in her class called "Just Between Us Girls": Towards the end of the blow job, you'll be moving your hand up and down so fast that your lover won't be able to tell the difference if you remove your lips completely. When you sense he's about to come, raise your head about half an inch. His eyes will probably be shut at this point, but just in case they're not, keep bobbing. When he comes, the semen will just dribble into your hand. Then you can switch hands and wipe it off on a towel (always keep one near by when having sex) or the sheet. If his semen really shoots out, it might hit you in the face, but that's still better than having to swallow it.

Timing is crucial, Barrows warns. So if you have trouble figuring out when your lover is close to climax, ask him to give you some feedback, explaining that it turns you on.

MORE MEMORABLE MOUTH MOVES

After you've perfected your fellatio technique (or even if you haven't), try adding the following erotic extras to your oral repertoire.

- Vibrate your tongue gently along the frenulum (the triangle of skin where the head meets the shaft) and wiggle it into the slit.
- Using your mouth like a vacuum cleaner, suck in as much of the shaft as you can. Then, still maintaining the vacuum, slide him slowly from your mouth.
- Try circling his penis with your tongue at the same time as you slide it in and out—not for the uncoordinated.
- Use your tongue to tickle his scrotum (the sack that covers his testicles) or *very tenderly* slip one of his testicles into your mouth (some men adore this; others find it annoying).
- Massage his G-spot simultaneously (see page 162).
- Nibble the shaft extra gently—but never, ever bite it.
- Use food to make fellatio more fun—and tasty. Spread on some honey, jam, chocolate sauce, whipped cream. Then eat him for dessert!
- Slip a spoonful of Pop Rocks (a candy that fizzes) into your mouth, then pop him in as well (a rather inventive *Cosmo* reader came up with this one). Also good for a thrill: let him share space in your mouth with an ice cube on a hot day, or a sip of seltzer—tingly!
- Pause occasionally, look up, lick your lips, and tell him that you hope he's enjoying himself as much as you are.
- Tie him up and do all of the above until he *begs* for mercy.

Want more ideas? Watching any porno flick (they *all* feature oral sex scenes) can provide additional pointers and variations on this ever-so-popular theme.

A Few Friendly Warnings

Though he may like to think of his penis as "a rod of steel," in fact, it's a rather vulnerable piece of flesh and needs to be treated as such. When erect, some penises naturally veer to one side, stick straight out, or even point down. Never bend an erect penis in any but its natural direction or you may cause great pain and injury.

In addition, despite fellatio's nickname, actually blowing into the slit in the head could be harmful (don't let him blow into your vagina either—it's even more dangerous). And it should go without saying that oral sex is out if you have a cold sore on your mouth or he has any kind of sore on his penis. In addition, it's probably best not to perform fellatio on a partner whose sexual history is a mystery to you, since it's possible that the AIDS virus can be transmitted this way. If you still want to indulge, use a condom. Yes, he'll be able to enjoy it almost as much. And you'll enjoy it much more, knowing that you're as safe as possible.

What to Do When He Loses You Know What . . .

"It was my third date with Jenny," Jeff, the 30-year-old graphic designer, recalls. "And the erotic electricity between us was so intense, I could hardly order my meal. Then when it came, I couldn't eat it. At one point, she took my hand, and started massaging my palm with her finger and I got this enormous erection right there. We got the check and necked all the way back to my place in the cab. I don't think I've ever been that excited.

"I was rock-hard until we started undressing each other. And I was thinking, 'Wow! She's so beautiful ... she's so sexy ... I hope I don't blow it.' I was trying to concentrate on making love, but I kept on wondering if I'd be able to give her an incredible enough orgasm—or any orgasm at all. And the more anxious I got, the softer my erection became—until we both looked down at the same moment and saw what looked like a peanut where my penis had been. I swear it seemed to have shrunk more than it ever had before. It was *horrible!*"

At some point in his life, every man is faced with the frustration of a penis that becomes and remains stubbornly soft despite its owner's desperate desire to make love. The causes can be emotional: performance anxiety, stress left over from work, the memory of an earlier lost erection.

Or the problem can be physical: too much alcohol, recreational drugs, even nicotine can make a penis droop—at least temporarily. Other physical ailments (such as spinal cord injuries, back problems, diabetes, heart disease, multiple sclerosis, or any other medical condition that impedes the nervous system's ability to control blood flow) and the prescription drugs your man may be taking in connection with them or other problems (including depression, anxiety, high blood pressure, stomach ulcers, and epilepsy) can also cause him to become impotent, which means he's unable to get an erection whenever you attempt to make love. In fact, according to Dr. Kenneth Purvis, author of *The*

Male Sex Machine, "Sixteen of the top two hundred medicines in the United States are known to interfere with erection."

Even too much time pedaling a bike can wreak havoc with your partner's penis because the hard seat puts so much pressure on the area. So if your lover's an avid—but impotent—cyclist, taking up a different sport, or at least buying a padded seat, will probably solve the problem.

The first thing most women blame when their lover's penis refuses to perform, however, is themselves. "He doesn't find me desirable," they worry. But unless you've dragged him to bed by the hair, it's highly unlikely that your attractiveness—or lack thereof—is even remotely to blame. If he didn't *want* to make love to you, he wouldn't be there. So stop being so self-centered—and figure out what you can do to help.

Whatever is standing between him and an erection, *your* attitude may be the most essential part of the solution. If you *sincerely* act as if a soft penis is no big deal, he's less likely to feel like a failure and more likely to become hard. "I thought all was lost when I went limp," Jeff explains, "that I'd open my eyes and find Jenny climbing out of bed with a look of disgust on her face.

"Instead, I got a pleasant surprise. 'Let your penis rest for now,' she said, smiling sexily. 'There are lots of other things we can do. I just love having my nipples—and other parts of my body—nibbled on.' Well, I was thrilled to have something to do that would give her pleasure, and I started nibbling like a maniac. She started moaning, and before I knew it, I had a throbbing erection—and the confidence to go with it. What a woman!"

If, like Jeff, your lover can't get it up because

he's too bogged down by performance anxiety or stress, a little erotic distraction may work wonders. Take the focus off penis-related activities and put his fingers and mouth to work on you. This is not the time to be timid, however. The poor guy is likely to be flustered and needs all the help he can get. So, like Jenny, you'll have to take the lead and suggest sexy activities other than intercourse.

Performing oral sex on you, caressing your breasts, even just some deep, sensuous kissing will take his mind off his problem, increase your pleasure, and decrease both your frustration levels. And making love in other ways is very likely to perk up his penis. Even if it doesn't, knowing that he still managed to give you some pleasure will salvage his ego.

LEND A HELPING HAND—OR TONGUE

If your lover becomes so paralyzed by embarrassment over losing his erection that he can't be easily distracted, you may have to take an even more active role in its revival. Sex experts recommend trying one of the following hand and mouth maneuvers (all work better if he has a good view of the action):

- Rub the area between his testicles and anus with one hand while massaging his penis with the other.
- While stimulating the shaft with your hands, use your thumb and index finger to circle the part of his penis where the shaft meets the head and squeeze lightly.
- Tease his stubborn penis with your mouth and tongue.

All of the above should be done slowly and gently—at least until he starts to respond (if he suspects you're frantic to get him hard, your efforts will have the *opposite* effect).

When To Call It Quits

If your endeavors fail to produce an erection within a few minutes, it's probably best to put it to rest (literally) for the night, unless your lover tells you otherwise. Just cuddle and talk *(not* about why you're not having sex).

Any kind of sex problem makes *terrible* pillow talk. If losing his erection is a rare occurrence, you don't need to discuss it at all. But if it's more than a temporary problem, you should have a chat about it. Bring up the subject at a time when you're both relaxed and in a good mood—and nowhere near the bedroom. "Try not to be accusatory," advises Dr. Zilbergeld. "Avoid closing in for the kill by saying, 'You always go limp when ...' Instead, tell him, 'This is my impression.' Most men will respond well to this kind of discussion."

A visit to the urologist's office is the first step in solving any continuing erection problem. Studies have shown that 90 percent of all impotence is at least *partly* physical, but only a doctor can determine if that's true in your lover's case. The good news: almost all cases of physical impotence are curable. In fact, it may simply be a matter of changing your partner's prescription for his ulcer to a medicine that doesn't drag down his penis.

If your lover wakes up in the morning with an erection, however, the problem is probably *psychologically* based. Luckily, this type of impotence is also curable, although it may take a little longer.

You'll find excellent advice and truly helpful exercises for this problem in Bernie Zilbergeld's book, *The New Male Sexuality: The Truth About Men, Sex, and Pleasure*, and Helen Singer Kaplan's *Illustrated Manual of Sex Therapy*, both of which are available at your book store. Or, if your lover is open to the idea, you could consult a licensed sex therapist, who will tailor treatment just for him.

As you can see, becoming best buddies with your partner's penis will help you cope with problems when they arise (or *descend*), and knock his socks off with your superlative techniques the rest of the time. And not only will your lover feel damn lucky to have found you, he'll also be inspired to become a stellar lover himself. The next chapter will give you both some new ideas to keep your bedroom repertoire fresh and frisky *forever*.

7
BEYOND THE BASICS

As you've no doubt figured out by now, being good in bed is more a matter of *attitude* than technique (although, as I mentioned in the last chapter, simply learning how to deliver a bodacious blow job is sure to secure your rep as a star lover!).

Still, once you've mastered the mindset, you'll want to move beyond the basics and add some advanced positions and maneuvers to your repertoire. That's good, because variety is the spice of great sex—and humans never stop craving more.

Even if you're perfectly content with your erotic routine, your man may not be—despite the fact that he swears everything is "fine" (after all, men have just as tough a time as we do making requests in bed!). As I mentioned in Chapter Five, he may simply go elsewhere in search of some sexual adventure. (According to former madam Sidney Biddle Barrows, 60 percent of the men who use call girls are married.)

Or *you* might be the one who's literally bored out of bed—even though you may not be completely aware of it. The signs? Maybe you and your lover are having more arguments than usual, you've stopped treating each other like treasures of pleasure, you're letting work, children, all your other commitments crowd out your time together, and you've sadly concluded you're just growing apart.

That may very well be true, but if you examine the situation more closely, you may find that the seeds of your discontent were planted in bed the day that one or both of you stopped making an effort to keep your lovemaking fresh and fun. As many couples discover, a long-term relationship and a dull sex life are a truly dangerous combination. For when the sizzle goes out of sex, it often goes out of the rest of the relationship as well.

When Rae and Martin married eight years ago, they spent so many hours having sex, they hardly had time to do anything else. "As newlyweds, we never watched TV and I think we only went to the movies once," Rae, now 32, explains in her soft Southern accent. "I would start to get ready to go out, but all I had to do was put on my black lace bra and Martin would be all over me. Before I knew it, the bra was off and the movie was forgotten."

A scant two years later, however, after their first child, Richie, was born, Martin and Rae's sex lives started to lose momentum. At first, Rae blamed the fact that they now had sex once a week—or less—on lack of time (a definite hindrance) and constant exhaustion (another legitimate problem). But as the months and years went by, their lovemaking remained sporadic. Even worse, the sexual spark that had once burst into flame whenever they so much as touched now seemed to have been snuffed out completely. When they did have sex, it was blah at best.

Studies have shown that getting married and having children are the two greatest danger zones

THE NICE GIRL'S GUIDE TO SENSATIONAL SEX

in any sexual relationship. Perhaps no one feels more overwhelmed by the demands of daily life than new parents. That's why clearing their schedules for together time is especially important. But lack of time and energy aren't the only culprits here. The wrenching psychological adjustment both partners must make to become parents can often stall even the most active sex lives. And because most of us never thought of our moms and dads as sexual beings, it may be difficult to imagine ourselves as both parents *and* lovers.

"I knew our sex lives were in a sorry state," Rae admits. "But I really thought that was just what happened to *everyone* after having a child." It wasn't until Rae, a restaurant hostess, became attracted to Bobby, a bartender at work, and began fantasizing about what it would be like to make wild love on top of the bar with him that she realized her desire for sex hadn't died out.

"My fantasies were incredibly exciting, but they scared me," Rae admits. "I knew Bobby was attracted to me too, and I was afraid that if he made a move, I might not be able to resist having an affair—even though I'm still totally in love with Martin and would never want to hurt him. Here I was, ready to risk my marriage just for a few sexual thrills, and that made me realize that maybe I should be looking for excitement in my own bed first."

So Rae decided to take action. She summoned up her courage for a visit to the X-rated section of the video store at the mall and bought *Sex Games and Toys*, an instructional—but still very steamy—video that's part of the Better Sex Video Series, which several of her friends had raved about. That night after their son was asleep, instead of watching "Murder She Wrote" as usual, she popped the tape into the VCR. "That program has gotten a bit stale," Rae told Martin, "so I picked up a little something new for us."

It didn't take long before the action on the screen heated up—and Rae and Martin followed suit. They began necking on the couch, a delightful throwback to their newlywed days. When a couple making passionate love in a bathtub came on screen, Martin said nostalgically, "Hey, we used to do that."

"Well, why don't we do it again right now?" Rae asked.

Martin didn't have to be asked twice. He clicked off the TV and chased his giggling—and highly aroused—wife into the bathroom. They turned on the water. But unable to wait for the tub to fill, they made passionate love standing up against the bathroom door, and both enjoyed the first of what were to be many powerful orgasms that night. It was the first time they'd had intercourse in anything but the missionary position for more than five years.

Like many couples, Martin and Rae had told themselves it's impossible to keep long-term sex sizzling. But that's not true. It just takes a bit more creativity and imagination to maintain the excitement that everyone craves. Buying a steamy video is a start, but Rae and Martin are going to have to keep adding new things—techniques, positions, sex toys—to their repertoire if they don't want to fall into another rut. For as any therapist will tell you, to remain happy—and faithful—a couple must not only grow together emotionally, but *sexually* as well.

Continued sexual growth is also essential if

you're single. It's almost impossible to make a complete emotional connection with a new man if you don't connect sexually. And for that, having a willing body is just not enough: you also need an open, inventive mind. That's what this entire book—and specifically this chapter—is all about.

If you're a bit timid about expanding your erotic horizons, simply start *slowly*. Just changing intercourse positions—and therefore the angle of your partner's penetration, the depth of his thrust, and the pressure on your clitoris and G-spot—can make a startling difference in your sex life.

The Prime Positions

Chances are, your lover has been spending a lot of time on top. The missionary position is America's most popular and may be your man's personal fave because of the total control it gives him. It may also fulfill your romantic fantasies to be pinned underneath him and taken by storm, but those fantasies better be pretty powerful because it's difficult for many women to climax in this position. When your lover's on top, it limits your freedom of movement as well as the clitoral stimulation you may desperately need to reach orgasm.

If he insists on doing it missionary-style, try keeping your legs flat and closed or placing a pillow underneath you to raise your hips. Both positions tighten the vaginal opening and increase clitoral stimulation. Or try this variation: sit on the edge of a bed, leaning back with your feet on the floor, while he kneels or stands between your legs. This position changes the angle of entry, which enables his penis to really push on your

G-spot and leaves your breasts free for extra fondling.

Better still, give your lover one of the following maneuvers to try, almost all of which increase a woman's chance of climaxing. Most men are happy (even thrilled) to try a new position for intercourse, so you don't have to mention your little advantage. Just tell him you "want to experiment" (words *every* man longs to hear!).

Woman-On-Top: Do you want it fast or slow, deep or shallow? You decide! This position gives *you* the control over the sensations you give and receive, especially if you ride your partner while kneeling or sitting astride him. By leaning forward or back, you can also change the angle of penetration, making it easier to ensure his penis hits your G-spot. This position is also recommended by sex therapists because the freedom of movement increases the chances of climaxing for a woman who's had trouble in the past.

What's in it for him? The chance to caress your breasts (swinging so tantalizingly close) and your clitoris easily. It also allows the man to abdicate control for once and enjoy being seduced. In addition, this position may help slow down premature ejaculators.

If taking control of the tempo makes you a bit self-conscious, try mounting your partner so you're facing *away* from him. That way, you can reach down and give your clitoris some extra attention—and he'll never have a clue! Many women also find they feel freer to fantasize while having intercourse this way since their partner can't see their expression, cutting down on the embarrassment factor. In addition, studies have shown that the angle of the penis in this position is almost perfect for G-spot stimulation.

Sounds like some pretty good reasons for at least giving this rear-facing position a try, but if you're still not convinced, keep in mind that your partner will probably enjoy making the most of the opportunity to grip you by the waist and pull you up and down on his penis. Many couples report they find this *very* exciting.

X Marks the Spot: Perfect for beginning a long lovemaking session, this position helps maintain arousal for a prolonged period, but probably won't push either one of you over the edge to orgasm. Begin by sitting on top of your partner, facing him, and insert his penis. Next both partners lean back in opposite directions, supporting their weight on hands or elbows (or lie back completely), and he then thrusts from below. When you want to switch to another position, either of you can sit up without having to disconnect.

Rear Entry: If your partner wants more freedom to thrust than he has when you're on top, doing it "doggie-style" might suit you both. To accomplish it, you simply kneel on the bed and allow your lover to enter you from behind. Not only does this position make it easy for you or your partner to stimulate your clitoris by hand, but because of the angle of entry, his thrusts are likely to hit your G-spot.

If you find kneeling uncomfortable, you can also lean over a large pile of pillows or a piece of furniture (the side of a bed, an easy chair, even a kitchen counter). Or you can lie tummy-down on the bed, using your elbows or a pillow to prop up your chest and head, and have your partner lie flat on top of you. But while this last variation puts a very pleasant general pressure on the vagina, it's almost impossible to find finger room to stimulate your clitoris.

Side-by-Side: If you're tense or tired, you can't beat side-by-side intercourse, a relaxing combo of cuddling and sex that's especially good during pregnancy (even the last trimester) because it puts no pressure on your abdomen. There are several variations. For the most popular, you and your partner simply lie on your sides in the "spoons" position, and he enters you from behind. Both of you can move easily and fondle your breasts, clitoris, almost *every* part of your body.

You can also lie on your sides, this time *facing* each other, with your legs closed and toes touching for terrific clitoral stimulation. Then, once you've enjoyed an orgasm, you can open your legs and draw your knees up on either side of his hips in order to allow the deep thrusting he may crave for *his* climax.

You might also want to encourage him to try lying side-by-side and face-to-face in the "scissors" position, with each of your legs alternating with one of his. That way, he can easily increase delicious pressure on your clitoris and the rest of your pubic area simply by pressing his thigh against it.

Sitting Style: This time you're both sitting—your partner on a comfy chair, bed, or perhaps the driver's seat in a car (use your imagination!), with you on his lap (an optimal position for G-spot stimulation). You can either face him with your feet on the floor, allowing you to set the sexual tempo, or turn to the side or face away from him, giving your fingers—or his—easy access to your clitoris. You can also try sitting on a bed and facing each other with your legs over his, allowing for a constant—and intensely intimate—embrace.

While it's true that sitting doesn't allow for much movement (in fact, you may have to change position in order for either one of you to reach climax), it's still worth adding this position to your collection because of the unique sensations you can experience.

Standing: While this may be the best position for a quickie (after all, it's hard to lie down in your host's bathroom at a cocktail party or among the boxes in the supply closet at work), be forewarned that, unless both partners are close in height, it takes a strong man with thighs of steel to pull it off (if you're shorter, you can help him by finding something to stand on and leaning back against a wall). Still, if you want to join the "Mile-High Club," use it in the airplane's restroom on your next long flight. It will break up the monotony, and your lover won't even notice his aching legs until later!

CAT: The New Pet Position

Many women, especially those who have trouble reaching orgasm through intercourse, have been raving about the CAT. That's not surprising, considering that Edward Eichel, the creator of the CAT (which stands for Coital Alignment Technique) claims this relatively new "clitoris friendly" method substantially increases even a previously nonorgasmic woman's chances of climaxing during intercourse.

According to Eichel's 1988 study of eighty-six men and women, published in *The Journal of Sex and Marital Therapy*, only 28 percent of his female subjects usually reached climax from intercourse alone. But that number zoomed to 77 percent after couples learned the CAT, and more than half began experiencing simultaneous orgasms as well.

So what exactly is this marvelous intercourse innovation? The CAT is basically a variation of the missionary position with two small—but key—adjustments: The man moves slightly forward on the woman's body so that the base of his penis presses against her clitoris, and instead of the usual thrusting, they *rock* together to orgasm.

This technique isn't difficult, but it does take a willing partner, a little practice, and some self-control (mostly from him) at least at first. Here's how to climb into the CAT (read the directions all the way through *before* you get into bed):

1. After foreplay, begin by lying flat on your back with your partner on top, and placing his penis inside you. His weight should be on his elbows.
2. Next, he should move into the CAT position by sliding up your body *about two inches*, so that his penis comes out of your vagina slightly and the base of it presses directly on your clitoris. Deep penetration is not necessary—or desirable—for this position.
3. Then he takes his weight off his elbows and lowers his chest onto yours, with his head and shoulders veering off to one side. From this point on, he must be careful that his

body doesn't slip back into the traditional missionary position, or contact with your clitoris (the whole point of the CAT) will be lost.

You can either keep your legs flat or wrap them around his thighs with your ankles on his calves—but don't raise your knees.
4. The CAT stroke is not a thrust, but a slow, gentle rocking motion that allows you to maintain full body contact—as well as delicious pressure on your clitoris—all the time. The woman takes the lead by pressing upward while her partner provides resistance, or counterpressure, to her movement. Then he presses down, while she applies the counterpressure. The movements are basically the same for both partners, and his penis moves in and out only a few inches with each stroke.

"The male and female sex organs together form a genital 'circuitry' that is complete when the penis is in the vagina *and* in contact with the clitoris at the same time," Eichel explains in his book about the technique called *The Perfect Fit*. "Simultaneous pressure and counterpressure during intercourse is critical to keep the penis and clitoris together, and to create a vibrating sensation that helps the man and woman to stay aroused."
5. For the CAT to work its orgasmic magic, *you must maintain the same motion and pace all the way through climax*—absolutely no speeding up, slowing down, or thrusting allowed! But this slow-motion technique can result in a *major* meltdown. While it may take a while

to get there, both your orgasms are likely to be more intense than usual and you have a good chance of experiencing them simultaneously.

Helpful CAT Hints

- Take the time to practice this maneuver, especially if you have trouble climaxing during intercourse. Most couples need several tries to get it right.
- *Control* your movements and position—if either one of you begins to thrust as orgasm approaches, if you arch your back or he slips down on your pelvis, CAT won't work.
- Conjuring up an image of his penis pressing on your clitoris may help you remain focused and achieve orgasm.
- If your partner is very heavy, he can avoid crushing you by putting his arms around your neck and taking a *little* of his weight on his elbows. But since the man's weight is part of what makes this technique work, take care that you still maintain full body contact.
- If your lover is very tall, he may have to veer off to one side more than a shorter man would.
- If—and only if—he begins to lose his erection, revert to the missionary position so he can thrust normally until he's hard. Then resume the CAT position and try, try again.
- Finally, if your partner has a very hard erection (lucky guy) he may not be able to slide forward those critical two inches since that move requires the penis to bend slightly. In that case, you'll just have to find *other* ways

to amuse yourselves (see the rest of this book for some ideas!).

Each of the prime positions mentioned so far is worth at least one try. While some may sound a bit convoluted (I'm supposed to put my leg *where?*), all of them are extraordinarily easy—and natural—to slip into. In fact, there is almost no end to the myriad maneuvers those with willing spirits can twist themselves into in the pursuit of erotic adventure. In fact, the ancient Indian sex manual the *Kama Sutra* lists 529 (!) positions for intercourse, but I find that number a bit mind-boggling.

In addition, the mysticism and meditation associated with Far Eastern sex practices don't seem to go hand-in-hand with really good sex. Treating sex as a totally spiritual experience seems to take a lot of the fun out of it. And the limits imposed on male ejaculation because of the belief that it saps a man's "life energy" seem a little silly, if not downright cruel. According to the traditional Chinese Taoist sex manual *The Master of the Cave Profound*, for example, a man should ejaculate only three out of every ten times he has sex. In exchange for this incredible self-control, he's said to enjoy radiant health and a long life. I think you can probably add massive frustration to the list.

That's certainly the way I would feel after participating in a traditional Hindu foreplay sequence, which, according to *Sexual Energy Ecstasy: A Practical Guide To Lovemaking Secrets Of The East and West* by David and Ellen Ramsdale, involves "repeated stimulation of female nose tip, armpits and navel in order before moving to genitals."

Instead, for those in search of more variety, I recommend a completely modern manual, *The Magic of Sex* by Dr. Miriam Stoppard. This excellent guide describes and illustrates fifty-nine intercourse positions, which should keep you busy for quite a while.

Or try creating your own variations. In any of the positions I've described (*except* the CAT), you can alter the angle of penetration—and therefore the sensations you both feel—by twisting your bodies a bit and/or changing the position of your legs. For example, you can add another spicy kick to the traditional missionary position if your partner simply rotates his body so the two of you make an "x," which causes his penis to press into the side of your vagina (this is different from "X Marks the Spot" on page 181).

In addition, keep in mind that if you pick a position you don't like—or even one that you do, there's no need to stay in it all the way to orgasm. Many couples change position several times whenever they make love. But beware of going overboard. As the authors of *Sexual Happiness for Women* point out, "Trying too many variations will tend to break the flow of your lovemaking and make it seem more like gymnastics than a tender experience."

A Private Tour Of Your Local Sex Shop

If intercourse positions are the meat and potatoes of lovemaking, erotic playthings are the garnishes that add a touch of whimsy to what might otherwise be a dull main course. Yes, you can do without them, but why should you have to? These grownup toys can help you practice safe sex, solve some problems (his too-soft erection or your inabil-

THE NICE GIRL'S GUIDE TO SENSATIONAL SEX

ity to climax), and add that touch of playfulness that *no* sexual relationship should really be without.

Too shy to shop? There's little need to fear. Sex boutiques have come a long way from the days when they were almost exclusively male sleaze centers where few women dared to venture (at least not without dark glasses). At Condomania, a national chain, groups of women giggle over the smorgasbord of condoms and sexual paraphernalia, and ask advice from the nonjudgmental salespeople. When I expressed interest in a mint-flavored condom, the man behind the counter cheerfully ripped a package open and held it out. "It tastes just like spearmint gum," he said helpfully—and he was right.

The atmosphere is even tamer—and much more serene—at Eve's Garden, a female-only shop in a midtown Manhattan office building that's about as intimidating as a bookstore. In fact, it's stuffed with books, as well as videos, vibrators, dildoes, sensual oils, safe sex kits, and all sorts of erotic odds and ends.

If you live in a big city, chances are there's a new-style erotic boutique like one of these nearby. If not, it's definitely worth sending away for Eve's Garden's mail order catalogue (send $3 to Eve's Garden, 119 West 57th Street, Suite 420, New York, NY 10019).

Unfortunately, shopping at a sex shop is not as simple as going to the supermarket—and it's not only because the latter is less embarrassing. It's often difficult to figure out just what an item is used for, and most women are too self-conscious to ask. In addition, the sheer variety of merchandise available can be so confusing (Eve's Garden stocks almost twenty different vibrators alone!), it's easy to emerge with the wrong product.

But you're less likely to make that mistake after you go on the following private guided tour of the average sex shop, complete with brand names, approximate prices, and the explanations and recommendations you need. So go ahead and browse with me. No one's looking ...

VIBRATORS

Faster than speeding fingers, more powerful than any tongue, often able to leap the orgasmic barrier in a single try, the mighty vibrator is a tireless climax tool. Depending on its shape and your preference, it can be used to stimulate the clitoris and sometimes the *inside* of the vagina as well. Although some are battery-operated, Dell Williams, the founder and president of Eve's Garden, recommends an electric vibrator for two reasons: the vibrations are stronger and it's always ready when you need it (batteries have an irritating way of conking out at critical moments!). Many women own more than one kind (the battery-operated versions are lightweight and smaller, which makes them better for traveling, although some women have confided that the handles of their electric toothbrushes can do double-duty in a pinch).

Here, according to Dell Williams, is the cream of the vibrator crop. Whichever you choose, remember that vibrators are electrical appliances. So keep yours *out* of water.

The Hitachi Magic Wand, approximately $40, electrical. This top-rated two-speeder provides powerful vibrations through a large, round, flexible, soft-vinyl head. If you find the lower speed too strong, try wrapping a towel around the head. But if the pleasure is still too intense (yes, it's possible), you might be better off with a less powerful battery-operated vibrator. (If you do experience any numbness, don't panic. Simply stop and it will go away.) An additional $7.95 will buy you a 4-inch-long penis-shaped "G-spotter" attachment, which is made by another company but is designed to fit on the Magic Wand.

The Body Mate Rechargeable Vibrator by Homedics, approximately $40, electrical, is similar to the Magic Wand, but has the advantage of being *cordless* and significantly lighter. It plugs into any AC outlet and provides thirty minutes of pleasure—as long as you're careful to keep it fully charged.

The Prelude 3 by Windmere, approximately $30, electrical. Though smaller than the Magic Wand, this baby's still powerful enough "for the woman embarking on a voyage into self-discovery," according to the Eve's Garden catalogue. It comes with a special attachment that can fit over the top of the penis (which the manual calls a "facial massager"—ha!). A 4-inch-long penis-shaped G-spot stimulator (see above) is sold separately for $6.

The Accu-Tone, approximately $20, uses two AA batteries. The round flat head of what the manufacturer calls this "personal beauty massager" is especially easy to hold and direct. Also included are attachments for body, facial, and scalp massage, which might just come in handy for *other* sensitive parts as well.

The Hitachi Mini Massager, approximately $20, uses one C battery. This unassuming tiny powerhouse, which comes with three attachments, is quiet but highly effective. According to Williams, "The tiny ball attachment drives men wild when you place it along the ridge of the penis."

Vibrating Balls, approximately $18, uses 2 AA batteries. In ancient China, weighted Ben Wa balls were all the rage among sexual sophisticates. Women wore the small balls (which are held together by a short string) inside the vagina, where they rubbed and rolled, causing constant arousal. This updated version comes with a separate battery pack to provide the added pow of vibration.

Some women insert these balls (or the old-fashioned nonvibrating kind) before leaving for a date or the office and conceal the controls under their clothing—a tricky maneuver that requires strong PC muscles (see page 51) to avoid the embarrassment of them popping out on the street while you're waiting for the bus. In addition, while this device will certainly be arousing, Williams warns that most women also need clitoral stimulation in order to reach orgasm.

The Pink Pearl, approximately $13, uses 2 AA batteries. Although it can be used for direct clitoral stimulation, this tiny, capsule-shaped, pink vibrator was designed to be inserted (a small cord attaches it to a separate battery pack). It's a good choice if portability (and *hide*ability) are key—and it's pretty too (something one can't say about many sex toys).

The Leather Butterfly, approximately $20. This relatively new contraption consists of a leather pouch attached to two cords, which you wear like a string bikini during intercourse (it doesn't cover the vaginal opening). Pop a tiny vibrator like the Pink Pearl (see above) into the pouch and the ensuing buzz provides much-needed clitoral stimulation *without* getting in the way too much.

But you don't need a partner to enjoy one. An adventurous soul I know told me that she wore her leather butterfly and pink pearl to the office one day when she was scheduled to work on a particularly stressful project. "Whenever I needed a break, I closed the door, turned it on, and had an orgasm," she explained. "Once, my boss came in and heard the slight buzzing noise, but assumed there was a mosquito stuck in the room. The fact that he had no idea what was going on was even more of a turn-on."

Joni's Butterfly Massager, approximately $18, battery-operated. Straps that go around your thighs and waist hold this pink rubber device in the perfect place for the nubby texture and inner vibrator to stimulate your clitoris. The soft, almost jellylike texture of the "butterfly" makes it easy to bear between your bodies during intercourse—or hide under your clothes while in public.

Ms. Silky, Ms. Smoothie, Ms. Mini-Flexy, etc., approximately $8 to $17, battery-operated. Although she carries these penis-shaped contraptions with dopey names, Dell Williams of Eve's Garden advises staying away from them: Customers report that they're too loud, the plastic's too hard, and they often break down.

Still unsure which model is right for you? Check out *Good Vibrations: The Complete Guide to Vibrators* by Joanni Blank ($5.50, Down There Press).

Sharing Your New Toy

Using a vibrator during intercourse can be an incredible experience, combining intense clitoral stimulation with the pleasure- and emotion-enhancing sensations of your lover's penis thrusting inside you, his lips on yours, his hands caressing your breasts. As long as you skip the missionary position or one in which you're pressed tummy-down against the bed, you can usually hold even a large vibrator between you (most woman-on-top and rear-entry positions are best). Or your man can do the honors.

If you find your regular vibrator too bulky, several companies make slim, flat vibrators (such as Joni's Butterfly Massager) encased in flexible rubber with straps that hold the device in the perfect place to stimulate your clitoris during intercourse—without covering your vaginal opening.

Nevertheless, if you plan to introduce your partner to your new electric pal, proceed with caution. As sexpert Dolores Haze explains, "While some men actually find a vibrator erotic, others might be put off by a large phallic object that guarantees you pleasure—and is not attached to them."

So don't just whip out your Magic Wand and plug it in without any explanation. Start by using your vibrator to give your man an after-work massage that's not even remotely sexual. Then ask him to massage you, so he learns how the machine works. He'll probably make the sexual connection himself and want to proceed from there. If he doesn't, you can gently suggest that he use it more erotically.

Even if he's not as skilled as you are in bringing you to orgasm with your vibrator, unless he causes pain, let him be in control of it the first few times you use it together (and don't plug it in *every* time you make love, or he'll become convinced you do like it better than his penis!). If he has trouble finding the right spot on your vagina, ask him to hold the machine steady while you move against it.

You can also use your new toy on your lover, but ask permission first. Your partner's entire penis is sensitive to vibration, especially the underside and frenulum, that tiny triangular spot where the shaft meets the head. In addition, applying a vibrator to the tip is so arousing, it may help cure a case of impotence. And if you want to give your lover a special thrill, place your mechanical friend between his penis and anus, where the vibrations will reach his G-spot, the prostate gland.

Still, as Joani Blank points out, "Vibrators have for so long been thought of as sex toys for women that some men react defensively to the suggestion they might enjoy using the vibrator for themselves." They might be afraid of seeming feminine or gay if they respond. Others are simply too physically sensitive to stand it. In either case, don't push the issue. Of course, on the other hand, your lover may become so entranced you have to buy an additional vibrator for him!

As I hope you'll discover, a vibrator is a wonderful erotic extra to include in any sexual relationship. After you've demonstrated conclusively that this is a sex toy you can use *together*, he won't feel threatened if you're the one holding it. But even if this mighty little machine remains your secret, you'll probably be glad you gave it a chance. More (electric) power to you!

Dildos

Most women say they need some kind of clitoral stimulation, even if it's very indirect, to climax. But while manipulating that tiny nub of pleasure may be what ultimately pushes them over the orgasmic edge, many experience an emptiness *inside* their vaginas when sexually aroused, and can't be completely satisfied unless that space is filled.

So what's a girl to do if there's no one around to fill it? Well, she can always turn to her trusty dildo, as women have been doing for thousands of years. These penis-shaped objects were once made of ivory, jade, silk-covered wood, even silver. Today, the best are molded from super-smooth silicone rubber, which feels more lifelike inside you because it retains body heat.

In response to a customer dildo poll, which indicated that women wanted a product that undulates the way no penis ever could, Dell Williams had several silicone models created especially for Eve's

Garden. Those in the *Venus Rising* series (ranging from 5½ to 7½ inches long and 1 to 1⅝ inches wide, and priced between approximately $27 and $45) have the wavy shape some women crave, while the *Scorpio Rising* series (5 to 7 inches long, 1⅛ to 1½ inches wide, approximately $27 to $40) point straight up.

Because dildoes don't provide a clitoral buzz, most women use their free hand to complete the job. Some even manage to wield a dildo in one hand and a vibrator in the other. Still others who are less well-coordinated turn to products like *The Eager Beaver*—a $37.50 vibrating and rotating dildo which runs on 3 C batteries. Topped by the likeness of a woman's head, this pleasure toy has an attached clitoral stimulator shaped like a beaver whose tongue vibrates at a dizzying speed—enabling the user to enjoy both vaginal and clitoral stimulation at the same time.

For those so inclined, there's also a similar product called *The Kangaroo* ($39.95) with a whopping 8-inch long, 1¼-inch wide dildo that weaves figure eights inside you while the little critter at the base keeps your clitoris busy. And $47.50 will buy you *The Great King*, which is the same as the Kangaroo, only bigger (9 inches long and 1¾ inches wide). If you're willing to spend even more (after all, who can put a price on sexual pleasure?), you can purchase a $55 gizmo called *The Rabbit Pearl*, which will do everything but cuddle and light a cigarette for you after climax. The shaft swivels and free-floating pearls vibrate while the rabbit's ears tickle your clitoris (got all that?). As the Eve's Garden catalogue says, "For the woman who wants swivels and jiggles and vibrations, this is IT."

While I find the thought of any animal—even a plastic one—having a go at my private parts rather alarming, don't let me stop you from experimenting. According to Dr. Judy Seifer of the Better Sex Video Series, "The sensations of a vibrating dildo in the vagina can be enhanced with a vibrating extension. [Using] the little tickler on the hood of your clitoris can produce intense sensations which often result in a powerful orgasm." She also advises starting such a vibrator on the slowest speed, and increasing it as you become more aroused.

Dildos (both vibrating and not) also come in handy if you or your partner would like a little anal stimulation during sex. Don't look so shocked—yes, lots of *straight* men find this sort of thing highly appealing. (Remember: the only way to reach your lover's own very powerful G-spot, his prostate gland, is through his anus.)

Still, don't approach your man wielding your favorite monster from the Scorpio series.

As you may have guessed, most sex shops sell a smaller, thinner dildo specially for anal penetration, but before you run out to buy one, first check to see if your man responds enthusiastically to anal stimulation with your gentle, *lubricated* finger (see page 162 for specific technique). You may already own all the equipment you need for this particular pleasure.

Sex Toy Safety

It's nice to share sex toys with your lovers, but don't forget to be smart as well. There's some evidence that a person infected with the HIV virus that causes AIDS can spread the disease by using your sex toy. So be sure to thoroughly clean all dildoes, vibrators, and other sex toys with ordinary household disinfectant or bleach—which destroy the virus—between each user. Or, simply roll a latex condom over the dildo or vibrator (if it's the right shape), and toss before anyone else takes a turn.

Massage Oils And Body Balms

Although you can certainly use baby oil, drugstore body lotion, even vegetable oil to give your lover a sensuous rubdown, paying a little more for a special massage oil is usually worth it. Dell Williams recommends the *Soft & Hot* brand, a condom-compatible edible oil which gets hot when you blow on it (ooh!). Choose from cherry, chocolate, lemon, raspberry, strawberry, even pina colada!

Rachel Perry also makes a deliciously silky massage oil in various scents, which heats slightly when it's rubbed in, and is carried in health food and many drugstores.

If you like to blow hot, then cold, try *Pleasure Balm* next, which turns refreshingly cool on contact. And that's not all. "Men love it because it helps them maintain their erections by contracting the skin a bit," explains Williams.

No matter which product you choose, remember to remove your best satin sheets before opening the bottle. Almost all these oils stain everything but 100 percent cotton bed linens. Even then, don't forget to apply a stain-removing stick to the inevitable grease spots before laundering. Or, simply have sex on top of a few large towels.

Lubricants

If you're ready for intercourse, but your vagina remains frustratingly dry (a common situation, especially after childbirth or as a woman gets older), a lubricant can certainly ease the way. *KY Jelly*, which is available in any drugstore, is water-based and effective, but so noticeably thick that it can feel a little too gooey down there.

A much better alternative is *Astroglide*, a tasteless and odorless liquid with the silky feel of natural vaginal secretions and the ability to remain on the skin's surface for lasting lubrication. Similar, but a bit more slippery, is *Probe*. Both are good choices if cunnilingus in on the menu, as is *Embrace Personal Lubricant*, which adds a taste twist with lime or strawberry flavors.

For easy gliding *and* extra protection against STDs, try condom-friendly *Wet Sensual Lubricant*, which contains nonoxynol-9 (an ingredient known to kill bacteria and viruses), as well as aloe vera and vitamin E (don't ask me why).

In addition, make sure that any lubricant or massage "oil" that comes in contact with a condom or diaphragm is water-based, *not* oil-based *(always* check labels to make sure). Any lotion that actually contains oil can weaken latex enough to allow sperm and the AIDS virus through. Even if there's no latex in sight, stay away from using oil-based products like petroleum jelly to lubricate your vagina. Yes, petroleum jelly will make you slicker than a greased pig, but it doesn't wash out easily and can harm delicate vaginal tissues.

EROTIC ODDS AND ENDS

French Ticklers are special condoms with bumps and nubs all over them. Prices vary, but they're usually at least twice as expensive as ordinary condoms—and sometimes twice as stimulating.

Although the inside of the vagina isn't rich in nerve endings like the clitoris, being "tickled" around the edge of the vaginal opening can be a real turn-on. Make sure you use another form of birth control, however, since these "novelty" items don't protect against pregnancy *or* sexually transmitted diseases.

The Kegel Exerciser ($69.95) is actually a little barbell with one large and one small end, which is designed to help exercise a woman's PC muscle inside her vagina. You "Kegel" while it's inserted (see page 50 for instructions), beginning with the larger end and moving on to the smaller one as you gain more control. You can also do the same exercises without this tool.

Why would you want to? Well, every woman should own a well-toned PC, since knowing how to move this little muscle at will can up the intensity of your orgasms and allow you to "caress" your lover's penis from the inside during intercourse.

The weighted feel of this miniature barbell makes it a dandy dildo as well, perhaps justifying its high price.

A *Clit Stimulator* is a flexible oval piece of rubber about the size of a kitchen sponge which is covered with rubber nubs and has a hole in the center. Your partner slips his penis through the hole with the nubs facing you so that they can tickle your clitoris during intercourse. Though it looks unassuming, many women swear by their stimulators (which can also be used on a dildo during masturbation), so it's probably worth the minor investment to check out its effect on you.

A *Cock Ring* can help prolong an erection or harden a soft one, but some of them, like *Extended*

Power, which adjusts to your partner's penis size with a screw, look a little too much like torture devices to me. Much more friendly looking is *Rubber Martin's Strap*, a soft, flexible sort of mini-harness that does the same job and can be removed quickly—a necessity if your man finds he is having trouble ejaculating with it on.

To put one of these products in place, you or your partner simply slip it over the shaft and behind the testicles while his penis is still soft. Take care not to pull it too snug since it will get tighter as he gets harder. Some rings have a little nub on the end designed to stimulate your clitoris and you'll need to be certain that part is in the right position. In addition, make sure you don't leave the ring on an erection for more than thirty minutes, or it could cause damage to the penis.

Harnesses are adjustable black leather garments which look like bikini bottoms and are designed to hold a dildo in place. No, you don't need one if you use your dildo just for personal pleasure, but it might come in handy if your man adores anal penetration and you want to play out a sex-role reversal fantasy. Still, I would make sure you're both into this sort of stimulation *before* you invest in a harness. It may look like a bikini, but you certainly can't wear it to the beach.

Restraints such as Velcro or metal handcuffs for securing your partner's wrists and ankles are popular, but expensive items for which it's easier and quicker to find home substitutes. Silk or satin scarves (or a few of his ties) will do the same job admirably and they're a lot easier on the wrists.

When He Wants To Try Something Kinky

Bondage, anal sex, golden showers, spanking, cross dressing, fetishes, public sex, group gropes. All are considered kinky sexual practices—and all are much more commonly practiced than you'd think. That's because, when it comes to sex, what's normal depends mostly on your point of view and what brings you pleasure. A woman might respond enthusiastically to being bound to the bed with silk scarves and "tortured" to orgasm, or indulge a partner's predilection for toe-sucking without a second thought, yet recoil in horror from his desire for anal sex, which *another* woman might find intriguing.

What should you do if your lover makes a "weird" request? Think *before* you speak (at least, if you don't want to alienate your lover). Many women feel threatened when their partners ask to try something out of the sexually ordinary. Instead, they should be glad that he trusted them enough to reveal his innermost desires—and they should treat those desires with the respect they deserve.

"To keep open the lines of communication, it's essential to be open-minded about the different preferences and attitudes that exist," writes Dr. Lonnie Barbach. "Withholding judgment on your partner's preferences doesn't mean you have to alter your own tastes. You needn't engage in acts that you find distasteful. To build intimacy in a relationship, it is important to refrain from labeling desires that are different from your own as immoral, weird, or perverted."

Give your lover's request some serious consideration, and be sure to follow what therapists consider the four cardinal rules of kinky (and every other type of) sex:

1. Know and trust your partner.
2. Practice safe sex.
3. Don't be pressured into any act you feel uncomfortable with.
4. If the sex starts to feel painful or wrong, stop *immediately*.

Never do anything you find degrading. Being an accommodating lover is one thing, being *used* is another. Some men insist on sex acts that humiliate or even harm their partners. And that's when even nice girls who are tempted to give in despite their misgivings have to have the courage to say no, loud and clear. Never let your partner force you to do things you don't want to do. If you do, you'll feel bad about sex, bad about yourself, and bad about him. And the longer you continue to give in, the more likely you are to do permanent damage to yourself—and your relationship.

If your lover asks you to perform an act you haven't tried before, ask yourself if you'd be willing to give it a shot once or twice. After all, you might find certain exploits much more enjoyable than you would have thought. Or, you may find his fondest desires no more than bearable, but decide to go along for your lover's sake. There's nothing wrong with that, as long as you obey the rules above and he's willing to accommodate one of your requests in return. Who knows? You could be taking the first step on an exciting erotic adventure.

By this point, you know enough about sexual techniques to bliss yourself and your partner right into orgasmic oblivion. But, as I hope you've also learned, great sex is about much more than just memorizing all the right moves.

As this book proves, to be a wonderful lover—the kind who knows how to give and *receive* immense pleasure—all you really need is the attitude that you *deserve* to have a fabulous time in bed and the willingness to do a little! That mindset will provide you with the energy and enthusiasm that make men swoon, the motivation to pursue your own orgasms without feeling selfish, the courage to communicate your desires to your lover, and the self-knowledge and self-esteem to say no—or yes—to a new erotic variation.

A super-satisfying sex life is waiting out there for you, but you must make an active effort to achieve it. Why bother? In the end, you have only one sex life, and it's *your* responsibility to make it the most rewarding it can possibly be. You owe it to *yourself!*

Look for These Other Books Coming Soon From

COSMOPOLITAN

September 1994

THE NICE GIRL'S GUIDE TO SENSATIONAL SEX
by Nancy Kalish

Overcome your inhibitions and enjoy
the fantastically fulfilling lovemaking
you've always dreamed about.

November 1994

WHAT MEN WANT FROM THE WOMEN THEY LOVE
by Ken Carlton

For every woman who has always wondered what goes on
in the minds of men,
here is an invaluable glimpse behind
that closed locker-room door.

January 1995

ALL THE GOOD ONES ARE *NOT* TAKEN
by Lisa Simmons

Plenty of terrific and *available* men are out there.
You just have to know where to look…
and how to attract them.